I CHING

STEPHEN KARCHER PhD is an internationally known writer, lecturer, translator and consulting diviner with over 30 years' experience working with the *I Ching*. He is the author of four translations and many books and articles on divination, psychology and spiritual experience. He was Director of Research at the Eranos Foundation, has taught and lectured widely in Europe and North America and holds a doctoral degree in comparative literature and archetypal psychology. He is also the author of *How to Use the I Ching, The Illustrated Encyclopedia of Divination, The Lover's I Ching* and *The I Ching Kit.*

THE SERIES

New Perspectives provide attractive and accessible introductions to a comprehensive range of mind, body and spirit topics. Beautifully designed and illustrated, these practical books are written by experts in each subject.

Titles in the series include:

ASTROLOGY
by Janis Huntley

BUDDHISM
by John Snelling

CHAKRAS
by Naomi Ozaniec

COLOUR THERAPY
by Pauline Wills

CRYSTAL THERAPY
by Stephanie Harrison & Tim Harrison

HERBAL REMEDIES
by Vicki Pitman

I CHING
by Stephen Karcher

NUTRITIONAL THERAPY
by Jeannette Ewin

RUNES
by Bernard King

SHAMANISM
by Nevill Drury

TAI CHI
by Paul Crompton

YOGA
by Howard Kent

New Perspectives

I CHING

An Introductory Guide to Working with the Chinese Oracle of Change

STEPHEN KARCHER

ELEMENT

Shaftesbury, Dorset • Boston, Massachusetts
Melbourne, Victoria

First published in Great Britain as *The Elements of the I Ching*
in 1995 by Element Books Limited

This revised edition first published in Great Britain in 2000 by Element
Books Limited, Shaftesbury, Dorset SP7 8BP

Published in the USA in 2000 by Element Books, Inc.
160 North Washington Street,
Boston, MA 02114

Published in Australia in 2000 by
Element Books and distributed by
Penguin Australia Limited,
487 Maroondah Highway, Ringwood,
Victoria 3134

Designed for Element Books Limited by
Design Revolution, Queens Park Villa,
30 West Drive, Brighton, East Sussex BN2 2GE

ELEMENT BOOKS LIMITED
Editorial Director: Sarah Sutton
Commissioning Editor: Grace Cheetham
Production Director: Roger Lane

DESIGN REVOLUTION
Editorial Director: Ian Whitelaw
Art Director: Lindsey Johns
Project Editor: Nicola Hodgson
Editor: Amanda McPartlin
Designer: Vanessa Good

Printed and bound in Great Britain by
Bemrose Security Printing, Derby

British Library Cataloguing in Publication
data available

Library of Congress Cataloging in Publication
Data available

ISBN 1-86204-763-4

CONTENTS

WHAT IS THE I CHING? 7

THE 64 DIVINATORY FIGURES 23

FURTHER READING 123

INDEX 126

Acknowledgements

I would like to thank the Eranos Foundation, Ascona, Switzerland, for its support of the *I Ching* Project (1988–94), Rudolf Ritsema for guidance, collaboration and insight, Luise Scharnick, Jay Livernois, Brigitte Heusinger von Waldegge and Ian Fenton, my long-suffering editor.

The publishers wish to thank the following for the use of pictures: Art Directors and TRIP Photo Library: 49, 54, 66, 84; Hutchison Library: 65; Mary Evans Picture Library: 7CL

Foreword

Thirty years ago, I was walking down a cold, rainy street not knowing where I would go next. I was alone, emotionally and spiritually in exile. I turned into a little bookshop to get out of the rain and saw a grey book with Chinese writing on the cover. An irresistible voice spoke to me. Later, when I used this book, I experienced what it was to ask a question and get an answer that said: 'I see you. I am concerned with your welfare. I care how you live and how you die.' That was the spirit of the *I Ching*. We could also call it 'The Little Book of Knowing What to Do'. Today, more and more people are turning to 'other' ways of understanding themselves and their problems. The *I Ching* is part of this. Consulting an oracle and taking its answers seriously puts you in contact with what has been repressed in the creation of our mechanized and de-personalized world. The *I Ching* gives you advice that leads to the personal experience of meaning, what the ancient sages called the Way or *Tao*. This is the real heart of magic. You can think about the *I Ching* in many ways and on many levels. The magic occurs when you ask the spirit to guide you.

WHAT IS THE
I CHING?

CHAPTER ONE

The *I* (pronounced 'ee') *Ching* is a 3,000-year-old book originally invented to talk with gods and spirits. It offers a way to deal with the problems you confront by keeping you in touch with the Tao or Way, the creative life we now call the unconscious. It can help you find your 'way' in life.

LEFT THE WISDOM OF THE I CHING HAS BEEN CONSULTED FOR MANY CENTURIES.

HOW IT WORKS

The *I Ching* is a set of 64 divinatory figures, each made up of a name, a six-line graph and a group of oracular phrases. These figures act like mirrors for the unconscious forces shaping any problem or situation. When you ask it a question, it produces an answer that can 'reach the depths, grasp the seeds and penetrate the wills of all beings under

ABOVE THE I CHING IS MADE UP OF 64 HEXAGRAMS – FIGURES OF SIX LINES.

heaven'. Listening to this voice enables you to work in harmony with the Tao or Way. It is a sort of helping spirit or navigational guide.

You don't just read the *I Ching*; you ask it a question and you get an answer. The answer comes through what your conscious mind sees as 'chance'. You pick six coloured marbles out of a basket, throw three coins six times, or divide and count out 50 yarrow-stalks. This 'chance' event lets something else do the choosing. It lets the spirit involved in your problem get around your conscious control and pick out one of the oracle's symbols to give you an answer. The *I Ching* uses these symbols to give you a mirror of what is going on 'behind the scenes' in your life. What you normally consider to be a chance event opens up the dialogue.

8

ABOVE USING PILES OF YARROW STICKS IS THE TRADITIONAL WAY OF CONSULTING THE I CHING.

THE MEANING OF *I CHING*

I Ching means 'Classic of *I*'. The important word is '*I*'. Usually the book is simply called The *I*.

You have probably seen *I* translated as 'change' or 'changes'. It really means a particular kind of change, when something strange or out of the ordinary is occurring. It tells you what you can do about it: be fluid, dissolve your fixed ideas, don't get stuck, let yourself be moved and changed by the hidden spirit. The symbols of the *I* describe the way spirits are moving in the imagination, spirits that are the 'seeds of events' in the world. The book connects you to these spirits and to your own *I*, your creative imagination, if you choose to use it. Those 'heavy problems' become gifts of the spirits, invitations to a dialogue with tao.

THE ORIGINS OF *I*

We don't really know where *I* came from. Many of the words of the book are at least 3,500 years old, part of a special language used by diviners and developed in the royal houses of ancient China. It grew from an even older shamanic tradition of songs, stories, chants and spells. About 1100 BCE, Wu Hsien, the 'Conjoining Shaman', put together the words, the lines and a way to consult them through counting yarrow-stalks. This was called *Chou I*, used by the kings of the Chou Dynasty to keep in touch with the Tao. People outside of the ruling family began to use the *Chou I* or Yarrow-stalk Oracle about 500 years later, during the Warring States period, a time of social breakdown and change. Society was falling apart, much like our own, and individuals needed the oracle's advice. About 200 BCE, at the start of the Han Dynasty, a group of scholars codified the writing and the oldest texts, collected the new material developed during the Warring States Period, and put it all together. The *Chou I* became the *I Ching*, the 'classic' of change. The book as we know it is virtually the same as the text produced more than 2,000 years ago. The text is still used throughout the East.

DIVINATION AND ORACLES

Divination isn't just fortune-telling. It is about finding and contacting what is hidden in yourself and in the world. Divination was used all over the ancient world to keep in contact with unseen forces. This gives the unseen forces or spirits a chance to talk to you now, here, in your daily life. Divination is a creative way of contacting spirit, of perceiving forces in the imagination and inventing ways to deal with them. What the old world called spirits are 'inner beings', or what modern psychology calls 'complexes' – centres of

ABOVE THE I CHING IS BELIEVED TO PROVIDE QUESTIONERS WITH A WAY OF CONTACTING SPIRITS.

power in the imagination that create what we experience as 'real'. Talking with these 'inner beings' and spirits heals, helps and empowers people. It gives them access to the great ocean of images and stories that the *I Ching* calls the Way or Tao.

Think about it this way. You want to do something and make plans. Then you feel strange and uneasy; you sense there is something going on. You need to know what the 'other people' in your psychological household think about what you want to do. Those 'others', the spirits or complexes, can either help you or seriously interfere with you. They know about things you are not aware of. They can warn you, redirect you, encourage you, give you instructions on how to go about things, or forecast disaster. The oracle opens the dialogue with these spirits, and the result of that dialogue is what the old shamans called *shen ming*. It means 'bright spirit' or 'intuitive clarity', or 'the light of the gods'. It is an awareness of the Tao or Way.

10

THE MEANING OF TAO

The word *tao* means 'way' or 'path'. Think of it as a great stream of living energy that moves and shapes the world. Tao offers a way or path for each individual thing. Where Westerners argue about logical definitions of what is real, Chinese argue about what the way is and how to keep in touch with it. It is the difference between saying 'I will find a way to do what I want' and 'There is a way for me and I want to find it'. In terms of Tao, it is the world that gives you the answer, not the other way around. Those things we tend to think are of primary importance – success, power, money, security – are secondary to finding your Way. Some Chinese thinkers said that Tao means a particular set of social rules. Some said

LEFT TAO CAN BE THOUGHT OF AS THE WAY OR PATH THAT WE SHOULD FOLLOW IN LIFE.

that it is a continual process in the imagination, a kind of shamanic journey. Some said that it is 'doing nothing' (*wu wei*), not initiating action but waiting until it is suggested by spirits or circumstances. But everyone agreed that keeping in contact with this Way is the most important thing we can do. The oracle was developed to help you do it.

To be 'in' Tao is to experience meaning. It brings joy, freedom, connection, compassion, creativity, insight, love. Someone who wants to live their life in accord with the way, and uses the oracle to help them, was called a *chün tzu*, literally 'child of the chief', the most important thing. The *chün tzu* doesn't just acquire money, power and fame. She or he acquires *te*, the power to manifest Tao in action and become who she or he is meant to be. For the *chün tzu*, the oracle is the symbol for a continual process of transformation.

CONNECTING WITH TAO

The first thing you need is a question. This question should grow out of a problem that you can't solve in the usual way. This problem shows where the spirits are moving in your soul. Look for the characteristic feelings: anxiety, desire, resistance, the sense of something hidden or confusing, the need for more or different information, the sense of something important pending. The problem doesn't have to be big. The fact that it draws your attention but stays hidden shows there is something deeper at work.

Making a question out of this problem has two parts. First, search out what you think and feel about it, who is involved, what is at stake, what you think it might symbolize, why you are anxious or uncertain, what kind of information you feel that you need. The answer will speak directly to these concerns. Second, formulate the question as clearly as you can. The clearer you make the question, the clearer the answer will be. If you can, come to a conclusion about what you want to do. Ask 'What about doing' a specific thing. Or ask: 'What should my attitude towards X be?' You can also ask 'What is happening?' in a particular part of your life or in a particular problem. For a real dilemma, ask twice: 'What about doing X? What about not doing X?' The oracle will offer you an image that connects you with the spirits or unconscious forces involved, the 'seeds of future events'. It will focus on you as the doer or actor. Be open to a surprise.

GETTING AN ANSWER

To obtain an answer from the *I Ching*, you first have to make a hexagram. This is a figure made up of six places that are counted from the bottom to the top. In each place there is an opened or a whole line. Each line is either stable or transforming. There are 64 hexagrams, and each has a name and a number. Each hexagram is also made up of two three-line trigrams, which also have their own individual meanings and symbolism.

ABOVE EACH HEXAGRAM OF THE I CHING IS MADE UP OF TWO THREE-LINE TRIGRAMS.

12

THE EIGHT TRIGRAMS

There are eight trigrams. They are all the possible combinations of three opened and whole lines. Thinking in terms of trigrams evolved later than the two kinds of lines and hexagram figures. It characterizes the desire for systems and synthesis characteristic of the Han Dynasty, the period beginning about 200 BCE that turned the *I* into a 'classic'. There are many associations with these trigrams. Later Chinese thinkers used them to amalgamate all the different methods of analyzing the world.

The trigrams also symbolize and invoke different kinds of spirit-energy. Each of the 64 hexagrams is seen as a combination of two of these trigrams and the spirits they represent. One of them presides over the inner world, one over the outer world. The oracle will give you a hint as to how these spirits are relating, so that you might understand what the tensions and possibilities of the moment are.

THE EIGHT TRIGRAMS AND THEIR ATTRIBUTES

Force/Field	Shake/Penetrating	Gorge/Radiance	Bound/Open

Trigram	Image	Action	Symbol
	Force Ch'ien	Persisting	Heaven
	Field K'un	Yielding	Earth
	Shake Chen	Stirring-up	Thunder
	Gorge K'an	Venturing Falling	Stream
	Bound Ken	Stopping	Mountain
	Penetrating Sun	Entering	Wood Wind
	Radiance Li	Congregating	Fire Brightness
	Open Tui	Stimulating	Mist

13

The meanings and associations of the trigrams are as follows:

Force, Chi'en: Force is a dragon, a creative spirit that lives in the waters and in the heavens. This spirit is a dynamic shape-changer. It can give you creative power and enduring strength.

Field, K'un: Field is the womb that gives birth to all things. This spirit nourishes everything; without it nothing could exist. It can give you the power to make thoughts and images visible.

Shake, Chen: Shake is the thunder spirit, who bursts forth from the earth below to arouse, excite and disturb.

Penetrating, Sun: Penetrating is the spirit of wood and wind. It is a subtle, beautiful and gentle spirit that permeates things and brings them to maturity.

Gorge, K'an: Gorge is the spirit of rushing water. It dissolves things, carries them forward and cannot be stopped. This spirit can give you the energy to take risks.

Radiance, Li: Radiance is the spirit of fire, light and warmth and the magical power of awareness. It can give you the power to see and understand things and to articulate ideas and goals.

Bound, Ken: Bound is the mountain spirit, who limits and brings things to a close. It can give you the power to articulate what you have gone through and make your accomplishments clear.

Open, Tui: Open is the spirit of open water. The friendliest and most joyous of spirits, Open brings stimulating words, profitable exchange, cheerful interaction and freedom from constraint.

14

You use the trigrams to help you identify your hexagram, once you have made it. The form of a hexagram is shown below.

THE FORM OF A HEXAGRAM

```
6 [     ]   Outer
5 [     ]   Trigram
4 [     ]   _____

3 [     ]   Inner
2 [     ]   Trigram
1 [     ]   _____

Number: _____
Name: _____
```

THE LINES USED IN MAKING A HEXAGRAM

stable yin

——— ———

stable yang

———————

transforming yang

——————⬯—————— ————▶ ——— ———

transforming yin

———X——— ——————▶ ———————

In each of these six places there can be one of four kinds of lines, a
stable yin line, a stable yang line, a transforming yang line
or a transforming yin line. All methods of making a
hexagram produce six of these lines.

LEFT THE CONCEPTS OF YIN AND YANG ARE IMPORTANT IN THE I CHING.

A NEW WAY OF MAKING A HEXAGRAM

Traditionally, there are two ways to make a hexagram: by throwing 3
coins 6 times, or counting out 50 yarrow-stalks 18 times. The coins
are quick, but the mathematical odds aren't accurate. The yarrow-
stalks are more accurate, in that they more clearly reflect the qualities
of the two primary powers, yin and yang, but the procedure is
complicated and takes up to an hour.

Recently, a new way was invented. It is as simple and direct as
the coins, but has the same mathematical odds as the yarrow-stalks.
You need a small basket or large cup and a total of 16 marbles of

4 different colours: one of one colour, three of a second colour, five of a third colour and seven of a fourth colour. Each colour represents a different kind of line. The one marble of the first colour represents the least frequent line, a yin line changing into a yang line (1 out of 16 chances). The three marbles of the second colour represent yang lines changing into yin lines (3 out of 16 chances). The five marbles of the third colour represent stable yang lines (5 out of 16 chances). The seven marbles of the fourth colour represent stable yin lines (7 out of 16 chances).

Now, shake and mix the marbles in the basket. Without looking, pick one from the basket. Draw the kind of line this colour represents at the bottom of your hexagram. Put the marble back into the basket, shake the basket again and, without looking, pick out a second marble. Draw the kind of line this colour represents in the second place of your hexagram. Replace the marble in the basket and pick a third time, again without looking. Repeat this a total of six times and you will have made your Primary Hexagram. If any of the lines are changing or transforming into their opposites, they will produce a second hexagram, the Relating Hexagram. Make this new hexagram

16

HOW TO RECORD YOUR HEXAGRAMS

6	[	]	Outer	[	]
5	[	]	Trigram	[	]
4	[	]	_____	[	]
3	[	]	Inner	[	]
2	[	]	Trigram	[	]
1	[	]	_____	[	]

Primary Hexagram   transforms to: **Relating Hexagram**

No: ____   No: ____

Name:_____   Name:_____

by changing the lines that were indicated. All the other lines stay the same. You can use the form below to record your results.

Now turn to the Key to the Hexagrams on pages 20–21. Look at your first or Primary Hexagram. Locate the inner or lower trigram from this hexagram on the left of the chart, and the outer or upper trigram on the row above. Where these columns meet you will find the hexagram number. Do the same for your Relating Hexagram, if you have one. Find the Divinatory Figure attached to your hexagrams, given in numerical order on pages 23–122. Read the Primary Hexagram and any Transforming Lines indicated in the consultation. Then read the first part of the Relating Hexagram, without reading any of the lines.

ABOVE THE 59TH
HEXAGRAM OF THE I CHING
HAS THE NAME 'DISPERSING'.

HOW TO READ THE ANSWER

The 64 Divinatory Figures or hexagrams appear in this book in a special way. They are all focused on 'you' as the one to whom things are happening, the one who needs to act. They help you find the most effective and imaginative way to deal with your situation or problem.

Imagine the answer to your question was 59 Dispersing (*see* p.113). The first thing to look at is the Name, the basic theme for everything that is occurring. The Keywords translate the theme into action and give you a basic strategy itself: 'Clear away what is blocking the light.' The first part of the text gives you basic images and directions. This comes from the oldest part of the original.

RIGHT 'DISPERSING' SUGGESTS CLEARING AWAY
WHAT IS BLOCKING THE LIGHT, LIKE DARK
CLOUDS BEING BLOWN AWAY BY THE WIND.

17

Then comes the name of the figure with all its possible meanings. This lets you feel the energy field you are involved with and all the actions it suggests. The next section gives you a summary of the commentary texts: explanations, associations, philosophical ideas and a sense of how the two basic energies, yin and yang, are acting. You can pick out what works for you. Then come the Transforming Lines. These sections combine the oldest texts and newer commentary. They are the 'hot spots' that tell you where and how things are moving and suggest specific strategies to deal with them. Read these texts only when a line in your Primary Hexagram is changing.

For example, if you had a Transforming Line in the second place of 59 Dispersing, it would tell you that in order to clear up your situation you should let go of things you normally depend on. You should strip away your habitual ways of looking at the matter at hand and let all the different aspects come into view.

When this line changes, it generates the Relating Hexagram – in this case, 20 Viewing, on page 52. Read only the Name of the Relating Hexagram and its basic texts tell you how you can relate to the answer as a whole. This indicates a perspective you can take on the problem, a possible outcome, a warning, or your desires or goals, depending on what question you asked and how you asked it. Here, the answer would suggest that looking into the situation at hand from a new and deeper perspective will bring the answer.

LIVING WITH THE TAO

No system of divination can tell you exactly what will happen to you, because time and fate are creative; they are continually moving and changing. What the oracle can do, however, is give you an image of the forces or spirits that are at work in your situation, and advice about how to handle it from the perspective of someone who wants to live with the Tao. This is information that you can put to use in your everyday life. Live with the images, carry them around with you and let them open up ways of understanding and dealing with your situation. The oracle shows the direction in which things are moving in the imagination. It opens a dialogue with the hidden spirits or the unconscious mind. The oracle does not tell time like a clock. It leads you into a story of time that puts what is going on 'inside' together with what is going on 'outside' in a meaningful way.

Live with the images that the *I Ching* gives you. Carry them around with you and let them open up ways of understanding and dealing with your situation. As you do this, spirit accumulates. There is a real presence in the *I Ching*'s advice. It can mobilize the deeper levels of your own spirit to help you find your way in the world. That's what an oracle does; and that is what this book is all about. This gives you tools, help, a feeling of contact, clues to avoid the worst kinds of mistakes and a sense of being involved with your spiritual evolution, rather than being cut off from it.

This book gives you the kind of information a diviner would use to help you see into your situation. Though it recognizes certain things as significant, it doesn't force you into a particular moral code. That's important, in magic, in divination, in psychology and in living. The diviner doesn't say, 'I know it all', or 'I am a superior person', or 'There is only one way to do things'. What the diviner says is that it looks like these forces are evident in your situation, and these are the kind of things you can to do work with them.

KEY TO THE HEXAGRAMS

At first sight the *I Ching* may appear to be complex and confusing. However, all you need to do is follow these simple procedures. To find the hexagram that the oracle has given you as an answer to your question, locate the lower trigram on the left and the upper trigram on the top of the chart. Then turn to the hexagram text that the number indicates.

LOWER TRIGRAMS \ UPPER TRIGRAMS	Force	Field	Shake	Gorge
Force	1	11	34	5
Field	12	2	16	8
Shake	25	24	51	3
Gorge	6	7	40	29
Bound	33	15	62	39
Penetrating	44	46	32	48
Radiance	13	36	55	63
Open	10	19	54	60

20

Bound	Penetrating	Radiance	Open	UPPER TRIGRAMS / LOWER TRIGRAMS
26	9	14	43	Force
23	20	35	45	Field
27	42	21	17	Shake
4	59	64	47	Gorge
52	53	56	31	Bound
18	57	50	28	Penetrating
22	37	30	49	Radiance
41	61	38	58	Open

THE NEXT STAGE

Once you have your question ready, and have made a hexagram, the next step is to turn to the relevant texts and read them. This is the kind of information and concern that you would get if you visited a traditional diviner or soul-doctor. You may be shocked at how directly some of it relates to your situation. Other parts take a while to sink in. Read the answer, think about it, enjoy it, take it with you. Step into it as if it were a costume or a role, through which we enter into the spirit of the unfolding drama and see what happens.

A good image for the process is that of throwing a stone into water. The stone is your question. When you throw it, there is a strong, sudden moment of impact. This is the feeling of intuitive connection that you will feel when you first see the text that answers your question. Then the circles of associations spread out in the water, penetrating into all the different parts of the subject. Finally, you feel the intuitive connection confirmed by this process of thinking and feeling through things. The water becomes still. The message has penetrated and subtly rearranged your imagining. You are ready to move with the way.

THE 64 DIVINATORY FIGURES

CHAPTER TWO

1 FORCE/PERSISTING, CH'IEN

**Keywords: Persist and create.
Make your efforts enduring.**

Force, the Dragon, describes your situation in terms of the power of the spirit to create and to destroy. You are confronted with many obstacles. Persist, for you are in contact with a source of fundamental creative energy. Continue on your path and don't be dismayed. Your situation contains great creative potential. It can open up a whole new cycle of time.

Force/Persisting, Ch'ien: Spirit power, creative energy; dynamic, enduring, strong, robust, tenacious, untiring; activate, inspire; heaven, masculine, ruler; exhaust, destroy, dry up, clear away. The ideogram shows moving energy, the sun and growing plants.

The hexagram shows creative force in action. Heaven moves and persists. This great force is the beginning of things. As the clouds spread and the rain falls, all things flow into their shapes. It shows the way energy moves in the world and the proper time to accomplish something. The way of force is to change and transform things and situations. It makes the innate spirit manifest. This protects the great harmony of the world. You can use this creative energy to inspire people and to give them models of transformation. You can create a source of a deep and self-renewing peace of mind.

TRANSFORMING LINES

Initial nine: The dragon is immersed in the waters below, hidden and secret. Don't try to use it yet.

Nine at-second: The dragon appears in the fields. Your ability to realize things is spreading. See people who can help you. Let your ideas permeate and organize things.

Nine at-third: A time of incessant activity. Creative energy is doubled. Active all day long, night finds you fearful and cautious. This change looks dangerous, but it is not a mistake. Turn your back on the past. This is the return of the Way.

Nine at-fourth: You make no mistake by playing. Dance in deep waters with ease. Your creative energy is most certainly advancing.

Nine at-fifth: The dragon is flying in the heavens. Your creative energy has found a visible field of activity. See people who can help you. Make things, build things, create and establish.

Nine above: Avoid arrogance. If you try to enforce your authority, you will regret it. This can't last.

2 FIELD/YIELDING, K'UN
**Keywords: Don't take the lead.
Nourish each thing and give it form.**

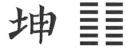

Field describes your situation in terms of the power to nourish and give things form. You are confronted with many conflicting forces. Yield to each thing, nourishing it and providing what it needs to exist. This will open up a whole new cycle of time. Keep your sense of purpose. Do whatever presents itself to be done. You will acquire what you desire and achieve mastery. Join with others in concrete projects. Put your ideas to the trial. Remain calm and assured. Don't take the lead. This opens the Way.

Field/Yielding, K'un: The visible world; the power to give things form; earth, moon, mother, wife, servants, ministers; supple strength, receptive power; welcome, consent to; yield, give birth, bear fruit; nourish, provide, serve, work for, work with. The ideogram shows earth spirits.

The hexagram shows an enduring power to yield and serve. Field gives birth to things. Its power to accept and give things form is unlimited. Reflect this through your generosity. Cherish each thing so its essential quality shines through. Be fertile and tireless. At first you will be confused, but don't be worried. Through yielding to each thing, you acquire new values. Joining with people can help you sort things out. Let your partners go when you bring things to completion. That will bring you rewards. Put your ideas to the trial. Accept hidden processes. Don't define things by setting up boundaries.

TRANSFORMING LINES

Initial six: Tread on the frost and harden the ice. Act carefully to establish a base.

Six at-second: You can establish things with ease. Proceed directly and sincerely. Focus on a single idea. You don't need to rehearse anything. There is nothing this will not benefit.

Six at-third: Act through a design that contains and conceals. Don't bring your part in things to an end through a need to be seen. Send out feelers in new directions. You will be greatly enlightened.

Six at-fourth: Bundled in a bag. There is nothing to praise or blame. What you desire is already there. Consider this carefully.

Six at-fifth: A yellow garment covers your lower body. Accept hidden processes. This opens the Way to the Source.

Six above: Dragons are fighting, sky and earth, beyond the city walls. Their blood is flowing. Don't let this go on. If you are responsible, yield, give way, restore peace.

3 SPROUTING, CHUN
Keywords: Help everything find the right place to grow.

Sprouting shows the beginning of growth, like young plants breaking through the earth. Assemble things and accumulate energy. This opens a new cycle of time. There are many new possibilities. Install helpers and establish bases. That brings profit and insight.

Sprout, Chun: Begin or cause to grow; assemble, accumulate, amass; establish a base, mass troops; difficulties at the beginning. The ideogram shows young plants breaking out of the earth.

The hexagram shows new energy confronting unknown risks. Clouds and thunder. Strip away old ideas. Let everything come into view. Set up structures that weave things together. This is a stirring time with heavy work to do. Things are coming at you from all sides in the dusky light before daybreak. Don't try to pacify them. This chaos is in accord with the time. Install helpers and give everything a place.

TRANSFORMING LINES

Initial nine: A large rock and a grave post sprout from the earth. Establish stable foundations. Install helpers. Your purpose is moving. You find an undeveloped potential that gives you great support.

Six at-second: Every time you start something, you run into obstacles and are unable to advance. Mounted on a horse fully arrayed, yet standing still. These frustrating things will not harm you. Negotiate alliances, though such a marriage will take a long time to bear fruit. This is heavy going, but in the long run the whole situation will be reversed. There are forces at work beyond your control.

Six at-third: Stop. If you go on this way, you will find yourself lost in a trackless forest. Someone in touch with the Way would stop at the first sign. Spare yourself regret and exhaustion.

Six at-fourth: Mounted on a horse fully arrayed, yet standing still. Actively seek alliances and marriages. There is nothing this will not benefit. Pursuing what you need will open the Way.

Nine at-fifth: You find the fertile juice. This opens the Way. Give everyone what they need. Don't impose your ideas. That would close the Way.

Six above: Mounted on a horse fully arrayed, yet standing still. This is bleeding you to death. Why let it go on any further?

4 ENVELOPING, MENG
Keywords: Don't act. You are unaware. Protect the hidden growth.

Enveloping shows staying under cover. You are immature and your awareness of the problem is dull and clouded. Accept hidden growth. Put the lid on. You don't really know what you are doing yet, but the beginnings are definitely there. You didn't ask for this problem. It asked for you. The first time the oracle will advise you. If you keep asking, you muddy the waters. Your awareness must change. This is an advantageous divination. Keep working at it. It will educate you.

Envelop, Meng: Cover, hide, conceal; dull, unaware, ignorant, uneducated; young, undeveloped, unseen beginnings. The ideogram suggests nurturing hidden growth.

The hexagram shows an outer obstacle that protects an inner source. Below the mountain a spring emerges. Energy is returning below. Turn back to meet it. The answer is already there, but enveloping means it is immature and has to be protected. Accept being visibly confused. Work on things gradually, like a plant bearing fruit. This is the season for inner growth. Use your confusion to envelop your desire to act. The obstacle is there to correct your one-sided view of things. When you understand this, you will become wise.

TRANSFORMING LINES

Initial six: Correct the enveloping. Restrain real wrongdoers, but don't shackle the energy you need to go forward. Let go!

Nine at-second: Turn enveloping into being responsible. This opens the Way. Care for things. Take a wife, support a household. Articulate your dwelling place.

Six at-third: Don't be grasping. Don't deal in idealized images of power or satisfaction. There is nothing of value to be gained this way.

Six at-fourth: Enveloping turns to confining. Isolation distances you from what is substantial. Correct your thinking. Return to the Way.

Six at-fifth: Young and enveloped. This opens the Way. Yield and work with it through gentle penetration.

Nine above: You attack what envelops you. Resist the temptation to break rules and behave violently. Yield and work with the situation. This you can connect what is above and below.

5 ATTENDING, HSÜ

Keywords: Wait for the right time. Attend to what is needed.

Attending shows waiting for and serving something. Find what is needed and wait for the right moment. You aren't in control, but you can provide for things, for you are connected to the spirits and they will carry you through. Illuminating the situation through repeated efforts will give you success, power and maturity. Putting your ideas to the trial opens the Way. Entering the stream of life with a goal brings profit and insight.

Attend, Hsü: Take care of, look out for, serve; necessary, provide what is needed; wait for, hesitate, stopped by rain; patience and focus. The ideogram suggests being forced to wait and the ability to bring rain.

The hexagram shows an inner force confronting outer danger. Clouds mount above heaven. Attend wholeheartedly to the needs at hand. Nourish what is immature. Eating and drinking together opens the Way and nourishes the spirits. Don't advance yourself. Spread repose, delight and harmony. Yield to precedence and persist. Don't think of this as an exhausting burden. It is acting righteously and connecting with the spirit above. It brings accomplishment and praise.

ABOVE HSÜ IS CONNECTED WITH EATING AND DRINKING WITH OTHERS.

TRANSFORMING LINES

Initial nine: Attending at the frontier. This is hard but persevere. It brings profit and insight. You haven't let go of your principles.

Nine at-second: Attending on sands. Small people and small talk surround you. Adapt to it. You can reach the source at the centre. Going through with your plans opens the Way.

Nine at-third: Attending in bogs, mired down and unable to move. This could end in disaster. Think about it, if you don't wish to be surrounded by outlaws. You can avoid destruction if you understand what you did to create this.

Six at-fourth: Attending in blood. You are stuck in a pit that may end up as a grave. Stir yourself and leave! You can be saved if you listen.

Nine at-fifth: Attending through taking in spirits. Join with others in eating and drinking. This corrects one-sidedness and isolation. Putting your ideas to the trial opens the Way.

Six above: Enter the cave. You will soon have three unannounced visitors. If you respect them, they will help you out of an inappropriate situation.

6 ARGUING, SUNG
Keywords: Argue your position. Don't act on it.

Arguing shows a dispute. Express yourself without escalating the conflict. You are linked to the spirits and they will carry you through. Don't be intimidated, but don't get involved in petty wrangles. Staying in the centre opens the Way. It is advantageous to see great people. Forcing completion closes the Way. This is not the time to enter the stream of life with a purpose.

Argue, Sung: Dispute, plead, contend before the ruler; lodge complaints, begin litigation; quarrels, wrangles, controversy; arrive at judgement, resolve conflicts. The ideogram suggests pleading before authority.

LEFT HEXAGRAM 6, SUNG, IS LINKED TO ARGUMENTS AND CONFLICT.

The hexagram shows a struggle with no solid base for action. Heaven combined with the stream: contradictory movements. This is not a harmonious time. It is full of people contradicting each other. Stay inside your group. Don't try to connect these things. Stir yourself and make new plans. You are connected to the spirits and they will carry you through. Don't be afraid. Stay in the centre. The time is against completing anything. See great people and clarify your ideas. Embarking on an enterprise now would be like jumping into an abyss.

TRANSFORMING LINES

Initial six: Get out of this affair. Say whatever you need to and get free. Be clear about this. Avoid a long and bitter conflict.

Nine at-second: Don't try to control this by arguing. Change your goals and go back to the place where people's doors are open to you. This is not a mistake. When the distress comes to an end, you can reap the rewards of your timely return.

Six at-third: Take in the power that comes from your predecessors. You are confronting an angry old ghost. Going through with your plans opens the Way. If you have been given a mission, it will not be accomplished. Hold on to what is important.

Nine at-fourth: Don't try to control this by arguing. Quietly turn away. You will receive a mandate from fate. Something important is returning that opens the Way. Don't let go of this chance.

Nine at-fifth: Present your case with confidence and expect positive results. This opens the Way to the Source and corrects the situation.

Nine above: If you think money and position will be bestowed upon you, by the end of the morning you will lose it three times over. Think again. This isn't worthy of you. It brings you no respect at all.

7 LEGIONS/LEADING, SHIH
Keywords: Organize confusion. Then take the lead.

師 ䷆

Legions shows organizing confusion into functional units. Put yourself in order. Develop the capacity to lead. Look at the people you respect, and use them as models. Using experienced people opens the Way. The idea is not to fight, but to bring order and protect others. It is not a mistake to use force this way.

Legions/Leading, Shih: Troops, army; leader, master of arms or a craft; organize, mobilize, discipline; take as a model. The ideogram shows people grouped around a centre.

The hexagram shows serving through a willingness to take risks. The stream in the middle of earth. Something significant is returning. Be open to it. You are surrounded by a confusion that will take concern and care to correct. This is not a pleasant situation. Give each thing a place. Support what is outside your normal values. Take risks and confront obstacles. Don't simply impose your will. People will spontaneously adhere to this. It opens the Way and is what is needed. How could it be a mistake?

TRANSFORMING LINES

Initial six: Legions issue forth using rules. Make sure this doesn't block essential force. Completely letting go of the rules closes the Way, but don't let them get in the way of what is needed.

Nine at-second: Stay in the centre of the legions. This is the leader's position. It opens the Way. The powers above give you a mandate that can change your life.

Six at-third: Perhaps the legions are collecting dead bodies – old memories and useless ideas. Get rid of them. They close the Way.

Six at-fourth: Legions go the way of peace. This is not a mistake. You haven't let go of the rules.

Six at-fifth: The fields are full of game. Be careful about what you say. Lead into action like the reverent oldest son. Don't act like the younger son and simply collect the bodies. This will close the Way. Don't tell someone else to do your work .

Six above: A great leader has a mandate from above. Enact your ideas. Found cities and distribute dwellings. Don't just adapt to things. You can achieve something significant. This may upset the way power is distributed. Don't worry.

8 GROUPING, PI
Keywords: Change who you associate with and how you put things together.

比

Grouping shows connections. Change your group and how you categorize things. Get to the heart of the matter. Find what you belong with. You can ask your question many times and the oracle will help you. This is not a mistake. It opens the Way. This is not a soothing time. Things come at you from all sides. Group them now. If you put it off, the Way will close.

Group, Pi: Join, ally yourself; find a new centre; order things, what you belong with; harmonize, work together, work towards. The ideogram suggests looking around to examine things.

The hexagram shows relationships dissolving. Strip away old ideas. Find new ways to group things. This doesn't have to be painful. Harmony, pleasure and elegance are a key. Early kings used this to connect the different peoples. Help each thing join with others of its kind. Connect your ideals with an underlying support. Take advantage of the profusion and change now, or the Way will close.

TRANSFORMING LINES

Initial six: Have confidence in your group. You are linked to the spirits and they will carry you through. This is not a mistake. Pour in more energy. Coming events will open the Way.

Six at-second: You are inside the origin of the group. Don't let the connection slip away. Putting your ideas to the trial opens the Way.

Six at-third: You are associating with the wrong people. Be careful or be seriously hurt.

Six at-fourth: You are outside the group. Use this position. Putting your ideas to the trial opens the Way. Stick with your work and your values. You are here because of your worth.

Nine at-fifth: Be like the king going hunting. Leave the game a chance to get away. Don't scold people. Let go of your predatory attitudes. Yielding and serving bring results. You are correctly centred and connected with what is above.

Six above: A group without a leader or a central idea. Leave now or face disaster.

9 SMALL ACCUMULATING, HSIAO CH'U

Keywords: Accumulate small things to make something great.

Small Accumulating shows what seems like a variety of unrelated things. Adapt to each to accumulate something great. Think of yourself as raising animals, growing crops or bringing up children. Be flexible and adaptable. Tolerate and nourish things. The rain hasn't come, but dense clouds are rolling in from the West. Successful completion is not far away.

Small, Hsiao: Little, common, unimportant; adapt to what crosses your path; take in, make smaller; yin energy.

LEFT HEXAGRAM 9, HSIAO CH'U, IS CONNECTED TO THE RAISING OF CHILDREN.

Accumulate, Ch'u: Gather, collect, hoard, retain; control, restrain; take care of, nurture, support, tolerate; tame, pasture animals; raise children. The ideogram depicts the fertile soil of a river delta.

35

The hexagram shows enduring force accumulated through gentle penetration. Wind moves above heaven. You need a place to accumulate things. Right now you have few. Focus on the inherent beauty of each thing. Be flexible and adaptable. Persist through gentle penetration and you will acquire a solid centre. Praise and let go of what you have, so the process can go on. The clouds are still spreading. It is not yet time to act.

TRANSFORMING LINES

Initial nine: Return to the source. How could that be a mistake? The Way opens.

Nine at-second: Something important returns, pulling you back like an animal on a rope. This opens the Way. Don't let go.

Nine at-third: The cart is stopped by the spokes. Trying to carry a big load brings on a family quarrel. Husband and wife roll their eyes. You can't order your home like this.

Six at-fourth: You are connected to the spirits and they will carry you through. Leave the bad blood and negative feelings behind. This is not a mistake. Your purpose unites you with those above.

Nine at-fifth: You are connected to the spirits and they connect you with others. Your neighbours have riches you can use. Take advantage of them. Don't go on alone.

Nine above: The rain has come. Stay where you are for now. You have honour and the power to realize things. Don't simply act as a wife. You will face angry ghosts seeking revenge. Be like the moon that is almost full. Don't discipline people. If you try to take control, the Way will close.

10 TREADING, LÜ

Keywords: Find your way one step at a time. Trust in the outcome.

Treading shows how you can make your way. Practise. Think about the right way to gain your livelihood. You are walking in the tracks of a tiger. If you are careful, you can partake of its power. Don't do anything to make it bite you. You can't afford to sneer and scold. The spirits will give you success, power and maturity.

Tread, Lü: Walk, step; path, track, way; follow a path; practise, accomplish; conduct, behaviour; salary, means of subsistence; happiness, luck; the paths of the planets. The ideogram shows walking feet.

The hexagram shows an outer struggle met by cheerful self-expression. Heaven above, the mists below. Everyone must find the right way to earn a living. Don't stay where you are. Treading is the foundation of your ability to realize the Way. Differentiate what is above and below. Set your purpose right. Clarify your relation to common desires. The stimulation you feel now connects you with a creative force, like treading on a tiger's tail. Your desire is solid and correct. Don't be disheartened. Continuing your efforts will bring a real change.

TRANSFORMING LINES

Initial nine: Go your own way, pure in your intent. This is not a mistake. You are moving with your desire.

Nine at-second: Treading the Way. Smooth things through continual efforts. Stay hidden and work in secret. This opens the Way. Your desire will not create confusion or trouble.

ABOVE THIS HEXAGRAM SPEAKS OF WALKING IN THE TRACKS OF A TIGER.

37

Six at-third: If you squint through one eye, you may see. If you limp, you may tread. But you can't see or act clearly. Treading on the tiger's tail like this closes the Way. It will bite you. You are a soldier, not a great commander. You don't have the capacity to move freely.

Nine at-fourth: Carefully tread on the tiger's tail. It listens to you and helps you. Completing this opens the Way. Your purpose is moving.

Nine at-fifth: Tread resolutely and leave old things behind. You will confront an angry old ghost. Take action. Correcting this is the right thing to do.

Nine above: Look at the omens on the path you have been treading. Your predecessors are extending their blessings. Following this path opens the Way to the Source. Your purpose brings great rewards.

11 PERVADING, T'AI

Keywords: Expand, communicate, connect, enjoy.

Pervading shows a connection with spirit that brings flowering and prosperity. Spread it by communicating. Be great, abounding and fertile. What is important arrives. What is unimportant departs. You have the chance to develop your ideas. The Way is open. The spirits give you success, power and maturity.

Pervade, T'ai: Great, abundant, prosperous; peaceful, fertile; reach everywhere, permeate, communicate; prodigious. Mount T'ai was the site of sacrifices made to connect heaven and earth. The ideogram shows a person connected to the Way.

The hexagram shows a creative force pervading the earth. Heaven and earth join together. Reach out and penetrate things. Radically change who you associate with. Serve the spirit. The fundamental powers are mingling with humans. Above and below come together. Your purpose is in accord with them. Be firm yet adaptable in your dealings. Stay connected to the Way. The way of people who simply adapt to advantage is dissolving. The Great Way endures.

TRANSFORMING LINES

Initial nine: Pull this up by the roots. It keeps you from advancing. Change those you associate with. Putting things in order and setting out opens the Way. Let your purpose take you into the world.

LEFT HEXAGRAM 11, T'AI, IS CONCERNED WITH THE SPIRITUAL CONNECTION BETWEEN HEAVEN AND EARTH.

Nine at-second: Surrounded by a wasteland and facing a river. Cross it on your own. Abandon your current relations. You acquire honour, for the centre of things is moving.

Nine at-third: After peaceful times come difficult times. But if you don't let go of what you care for, it will never be able to return. You are facing a difficult task. This is not a mistake. You are connected to the spirits and they will carry you through. Eat and drink with others on the path. What is coming will bring you blessings.

Six at-fourth: You flutter like a little bird leaving the nest. If you don't have the resources, call on your family or friends. You are connected to the spirits and they will carry you through. Centre and stabilize your heart's desires.

Six at-fifth: The Great Ancestor marries a maiden, omen of future happiness. This gratifies desires and fulfils your aims. It opens the Way to the Source. Use this to act on your ideas, but wait for the right moment.

Six above: The walls collapse into the moat. The city falls. Don't organize your troops to combat it. Notify your own people, for this has fate behind it. Putting your ideas to the trial now only brings shame and confusion. Your destiny is in disarray.

12 OBSTRUCTION, PI
Keywords: Stop! Beware, communication is blocked.

Obstruction shows someone blocked or interfered with. Stop and accept it. Communication is cut off. You are connected with the wrong people. If you try to act, the

RIGHT THE 12TH HEXAGRAM OFTEN INDICATES A WARNING.

Way will close. There is no advantage in this situation. What is important departs, what arrives is small and mean. Don't try to impose your ideas. You will certainly fail.

Obstruct, Pi: Closed, stopped, bar the way; obstacle; unable to advance; deny, refuse, disapprove; bad, evil, unfortunate, wicked, unhappy. The ideogram suggests blocked communication.

The hexagram shows a struggle that blocks expression. Heaven and earth do not join together. Change those you associate with. Don't mingle. If you avoid responsibility and self-display, you can continue to benefit from the situation. This is not your fault. It is a time of disconnection and isolation. Be humble and flexible, but erect firm barriers. What is worthy is excluded by people who seek their own advantage. Their way endures for now. The Great Way dissolves. Diminish your involvements. They bring you no advantage.

40

TRANSFORMING LINES

Initial six: Pull this up by the roots. It is twisted and confused and keeps you tied to the situation. Change those you associate with. Putting your ideas to the trial opens the way. Follow what you believe in.

Six at-second: Wrap up what you receive. Adapt to what crosses your path. This opens the Way. You are obstructed, but your ideas are growing. Make an offering. The spirits can give you success, power and maturity in the end. Don't make the people around you nervous about you.

Six at-third: Taking responsibility now will only embarrass you. Don't do it. Avoid gifts and honours.

Nine at-fourth: A mandate from fate. Continue on through obstruction and isolation. In the end you will experience great happiness and spread light and awareness. There is no mistake here. Your purpose is moving.

Nine at-fifth: Let the obstructions go. Take a break. Relax and withdraw. This opens the Way. The bad time is ending. Imagine yourself in a peaceful and luxuriant rural retreat. This is the right place for you. Relax and enjoy yourself.

Nine above: The obstruction is turned on its head. What was a block is now cause for rejoicing. The bad time is over. Why go on regretting things? Let go and join the celebration.

13 CONCORDING PEOPLE, T'UNG JEN

Keywords: Assemble, co-operate, unite for a common goal.

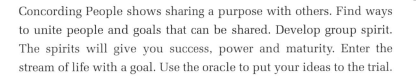

Concording People shows sharing a purpose with others. Find ways to unite people and goals that can be shared. Develop group spirit. The spirits will give you success, power and maturity. Enter the stream of life with a goal. Use the oracle to put your ideas to the trial.

Concord, T'ung: Harmonize, bring together, unite; union, concord; assemble, share, agree; held in common. The ideogram suggests silent understanding.

People, Jen: Human beings; an individual; humanity. The ideogram shows a person kneeling.

RIGHT HEXAGRAM 13, T'UNG JEN, IS LINKED TO HARMONIOUS RELATIONSHIPS.

The hexagram shows warmth and understanding that help people in their struggles. Heaven unites with fire. People should not remain isolated. Think about ways to connect them. Give them rallying points and common ancestors. Be flexible and adaptable. Say it like this: Bring people together, for creative force is moving. Try to illuminate the inherent beauty of things. Don't go to extremes. You can connect with the deep purposes that move the human world.

TRANSFORMING LINES

Initial nine: People gather at the gate, about to cross over the threshold. This is not a mistake. Walk through the door. Where is the fault in that?

Six at-second: People gather in the ancestral hall and feel the shame and confusion of having lost the Way. This is the right feeling. Let this induce reflection and correct how you are thinking.

Nine at-third: Hide your weapons in the thick undergrowth. Climb to the tombs of your ancestors, where you can think about things and find help. Avoid resentment. You are facing a very strong antagonist. You will not be able to act for quite a while.

Nine at-fourth: Ride on your ramparts. No one can attack or control you. Stimulate vital power and desire. This opens the Way and reverses a confining situation.

Nine at-fifth: People who gather cry and wail, then laugh and rejoice. Having a cause unites them. Speak plainly and sincerely. Using words well can bring this group together.

Nine above: People gather at the city's edge. There is no cause for sorrow, but this group doesn't have a purpose yet. Take action. You are coupled with a creative force.

14 GREAT POSSESSING, TA YU

Keywords: A time to be great. Concentrate, produce and share the results.

Great Possessing shows abundance through having a central idea. Concentrate your energies and share the fruits of your efforts. This is a source of fertility and excellence. The spirits will give you success, power maturity. Make them an offering and share their gifts with others.

Great, Ta: Big, noble, important; able to protect others; orient your will towards a self-imposed goal; lead or guide your life; yang energy.

Possess, Yu: There is; to be, to exist; have, own; possessions, goods. The ideogram suggests sharing with the spirits and other people.

The hexagram shows an inner force spreading brightness and warmth. Fire above heaven. Be resolute. Associate with people and convert them to your idea. Firmly check hatred and bring out what is virtuous. Work with the spirit above and let go of your personal limits. Your idea will come to the centre of attention. Above and below respond to it. This is great possessing. You realize the Way and brighten the inherent beauty of things. This connects you with heaven and the right time to act. The spirits give you success, power and maturity.

TRANSFORMING LINES

Initial nine: There is no harm in this. It is not a mistake. The hard work involved is not a mistake, but the beginning of a great endeavour.

43

RIGHT THE 14TH HEXAGRAM IS CONCERNED WITH CONCENTRATION OF ENERGY AND MIND.

Nine at-second: Use a great vehicle to carry your ideas. Have a firm direction. This is not a mistake. Amass strength in the centre. There is no harm in this.

Nine at-third: Concentrate what you have grown. Present it to the highest principle, like a noble making a gift to the Son of Heaven. This creates a firm connection. Don't let small concerns control your ideas. That would be harmful now.

Nine at-fourth: Don't try to dominate. Be very clear about this. Share things. Let others shine. This is not a mistake.

Six at-fifth: The spirits are certainly with you! You simply meet people and you impress them. The spirits will carry you through. The Way is open. Stay true to your ideas. Your power has real meaning. Be versatile instead of trying to prepare things.

Nine above: Heaven shields and protects you. There is nothing that this will not benefit. Your idea has great significance. It is protected and blessed by the spirit.

15 HUMBLING, CH'IEN
Keywords: Think and speak humbly to accomplish your goals.

Humbling shows cutting through pride and complication. Keep your words simple and connected to facts. Think of yourself in a modest way. The spirits will give you success, power and maturity. You can bring things to completion. Humbling brings a great power of realization. Be clear about this, then act directly.

Humble, Ch'ien: Think and speak in a modest way; give way to others, polite, modest, simple, respectful; yielding, compliant, reverent. The ideogram suggests keeping words connected to facts.

The hexagram shows an inner limit that connects you to the earth. In the middle of earth, a mountain. Don't go to extremes. Be agile and alert. Humbling gives you the power to be who you are meant to be. It dignifies and clarifies things. Reduce the many to augment the few. Heaven moves below, bringing brightness and clarity. Earth moves above. Heaven lessens what is overfull and augments the humble. Earth transforms what is overfull and spreads the humble. Souls and spirits harm what is overfull and bless the humble. People hate what is overfull and love the humble. Humbling does not try to go beyond what is there. Through it you accomplish things.

ABOVE THE 15TH HEXAGRAM SPEAKS OF THE INFLUENCE OF HEAVEN ON EARTH ON THE HUMBLE.

TRANSFORMING LINES

Initial six: Be very humble. Think everything through twice. Then step into the stream of life with a purpose. The Way is open to you.

45

Six at-second: Let your power speak humbly and call out to others. Putting your ideas to the trial opens the Way. Make a heartfelt statement and you can obtain what you wish.

Nine at-third: Humbly carry on. Exert yourself without advertising. Completing things opens the Way. It mobilizes an undeveloped potential that will attract many people.

Six at-fourth: There is nothing that this will not benefit. Simply show your ideas. Don't argue or impose your will.

Six at-fifth: Take action. If you don't have the resources, use your neighbour's. Invade and subjugate things by whatever means necessary. There is nothing that this will not benefit. The time is right. Discipline and put things in order.

Six above: Let your power speak humbly and call out to others. Mobilize your forces and attack. You haven't acquired what you need. The time is right to get it.

16 PROVIDING FOR, YÜ
Keywords: Prepare now. You will enjoy it later.

豫

Providing for shows gathering what is needed to meet the future. Accumulate strength so that you can respond spontaneously and move smoothly with the flow of events. Empowering helpers to mobilize your forces brings profit and insight.

Provide for, Yü: Prepared, take precautions, arrange, make ready; happy, content, rejoice, take pleasure; enthusiastic, spontaneous. The ideogram suggests that being prepared enables you to be spontaneous.

The hexagram shows accumulated energy bounding forth. Thunder comes from earth impetuously. Humbly amass a great store to provide for what comes. Double the gates and establish the watch so you are ready for violent visitors. When thunder burst from the earth, Early Kings aroused delight and made music to realize the Way. They exalted the spirit and became very wise. Build the capacity to spontaneously respond. Establish helpers to mobilize your forces. This is how heaven and earth work together. The old wise people could respond immediately from their store of power. The time of providing for is righteous and great.

LEFT THE FIGURE YU IS CONNECTED WITH HAPPINESS AND ENTHUSIASM.

Transforming Lines

Initial six: Don't call on others to build up what you need. You will be cut off from the spirits and left open to danger. The Way will close and your purpose be exhausted. Wait and respond to a real stimulus.

Six at-second: The limits you have set are turning you to stone. Leave this situation. Don't complete even one more day. The Way is open. Make correcting your position your central concern.

Six at-third: Don't be sceptical and don't procrastinate. Provide for what is needed now or you will most certainly be sorry.

Nine at-fourth: Have no doubts. You acquire what you desire. You join people together like cowries strung on a thread. Your purpose moves great things.

Six at-fifth: You are confronting affliction, sickness or hatred. Keep on. It won't kill you. You are riding a creative force.

47

Six above: You are groping in the dark. Let go of what is past. The situation isn't your fault, but why let it go on any longer? Climb out of the cave of past experience.

17 FOLLOWING, SUI
Keywords: Don't fight it.
Go with the flow.

Following shows being effortlessly drawn forward. Follow the inevitable course of events. Go with the flow. Yield to the path set out in front of you. Be guided by the way things are moving. You are involved in a series of events that are firmly connected. Don't fight it, move with it. It opens a whole new cycle of time. This is not a mistake. The situation cannot harm you. The spirits will give you success, power and maturity.

Follow, Sui: Come or go after in inevitable sequence; conform to, according to; in the style of, according to the ideas of, the same direction; follow a way, school or religion. The ideogram shows one step following another.

The hexagram shows an outer stimulus rousing inner energy. Thunder in the middle of the mists. When you have provided for the call, it comes. Let go of what is past. Dim your discriminating power so old mental habits dissolve. A new focus is emerging. The spirits will give you success, power and maturity. This is not a mistake. The human world must follow the times and the seasons. What you follow here is a righteous idea inherent in the time.

TRANSFORMING LINES

Initial nine: Deny the position you have and go out through the gate. Leave your beliefs behind. The Way is open. Mingling with others gets real work done.

Six at-second: Attached to the small child, you let the responsible manager go. You must adapt to whatever crosses your path.

Six at-third: Attached to the responsible manager, you let the small child go. Through following this path you will seek and acquire what you desire. Continuing will bring profit and insight. Have a firm purpose.

Nine at-fourth: You are following simply in order to catch something. The Way closes. Think about this and change your approach. Following the Way will brighten your awareness. This links you to the spirits and they will carry you through. How could that be a mistake? Your righteousness is leading you astray.

Nine at-fifth: You are linked to the spirits and they will carry you through, moving you towards real excellence. The Way is open.

Six above: You are firmly attached to what you follow. Through you, others are held together. You become one of the ancestral spirits.

18 CORRUPTION/ RENOVATING, KU
Keywords: Beware! Search out the source of corruption.

Corruption shows poison, putrefaction, black magic and the evil deeds done by parents manifested in their children. Find a new beginning. Search out the source so new growth can begin. The spirits will give you success, power and maturity. Entering the stream of life with a goal brings profit and insight. Prepare the moment and watch over its growth: three days before the seed sprouts and three days to stabilize growth.

Corrupt/Renovating, Ku: Rotting, poisonous; intestinal worms, venomous insects, evil magic; seduce, pervert, flatter, put under a spell; disorder, error; business. The ideogram shows poisonous insects in a jar used for magic.

49

The hexagram shows an obstacle that turns inner growth back on itself. The wind below the mountain. Doing business always implies corruption. Find its source and you can stabilize the situation. Rouse

undeveloped potential. A limit above is stopping new growth: corruption. This is the chance for a new beginning. Make the effort. The spirits will give you success, power and maturity. Set out with a firm

LEFT THE 18TH HEXAGRAM IS CONNECTED WITH PUTREFACTION AND POISON, PARTICULARLY VENOMOUS INSECTS.

purpose. You will soon be busy. Take three days before the new seed bursts and three days afterwards. Watch carefully. The spirit above is moving in this.

TRANSFORMING LINES

Initial six: Dealing with a father's corruption in exercising authority. Accept being a son. Consult with the wise old men. This is not a mistake. You are facing a difficult time. You are facing an old angry ghost. Going through this opens the Way. Examine how gifts were received and how orders were carried out. Clear this up and your predecessors remain without fault.

Nine at-second: Dealing with a mother's corruption in nourishing children. Divination can't help you. Find the centre of the situation and put yourself in the Way and the answer will come of itself.

Nine at-third: Dealing with a father's corruption in exercising authority. You will regret it if you simply adapt. Have your own ideas and bring things to completion.

Six at-fourth: Adding to the father's corruption. If you go on like this, you will be covered with shame and confusion.

Six at-fifth: Dealing with a father's corruption in exercising authority. Use praise to handle the situation. You gain the power to realize your own destiny.

Nine above: Business and politics are not your job. Your purpose is to find what is excellent. This is the place of those who work to provide for a coming awakening.

19 NEARING, LIN
Keywords: The point of new arrival.
Welcome what is approaching.

Nearing shows something great approaching something smaller, the point of new contact. Accept it without expecting to immediately get what you want. Look at things with care and sympathy. Keep your expectations modest. This contact opens a whole new cycle of time. Trying to rush to an early harvest will close the Way.

Nearing, Lin: Approach, behold with care, come nearer; confer favour and blessing; arrive, make contact; honour or be honoured by a visit.

The hexagram invites contact through a willingness to work and serve. Earth above the mists. This is the return of the great. Invite it to come nearer. When you teach, continually ponder the heart's concerns. Tolerate and protect things without limit. What is strong and firm increases gradually. Stay centred and connected. If you want something great, you must continually correct yourself. That is heaven's way. Rushing to an early harvest closes the Way.

TRANSFORMING LINES

Initial nine: An inspiring connection comes nearer. It connects things that belong together. The Way is open. Your purpose is moving.

Nine at-second: An inspiring connection comes nearer. It connects things that belong together. The Way is open. There is nothing this will not benefit.

Six at-third: Something sweet comes nearer. There is no way good can come of it. If you have already realized this, no lasting harm will result.

RIGHT THE 19TH HEXAGRAM MAY INDICATE THE APPROACH OF GOOD FORTUNE.

Six at-fourth: The climax comes nearer. This is not a mistake. The time is right. Go for it.

Six at-fifth: Knowledge comes nearer that belongs to a great chief. The way is open. This can change the way you see everything.

Six above: Wealth and generosity come nearer. The Way is open. It is not a mistake. Hold on to your inner purpose.

20 VIEWING, KUAN
Keywords: Let everything come into view. Divine the meaning.

Viewing shows looking without acting. Let everything emerge and divine the meaning. Look at what you usually don't want to see. This is like the moment in a ceremony when the purification has been made and the libation is poured out. Examining things will bring you the insight you need. The spirit will arrive and carry you through.

View, Kuan: Contemplate, look at from a distance or height; judge, divine the meaning; instruct, inform, point out, make known; a Taoist monastery, an observatory. The ideogram suggests a bird's-eye view and watching bird signs.

The hexagram shows images appearing on the inner field. Wind moves above earth. Strip away your old ideas. There is something of great importance here. Early kings used this time to inspect the borders, contemplate the people's needs and set up teaching. Yield to things and give them space on the inner

LEFT THIS HEXAGRAM SUGGESTS VIEWING FROM A DISTANCE.

ground. Let the whole world come into view. The spirit will answer and carry you through. Things will change spontaneously. By viewing the way heaven moves, you see the proper time to act. When the sages used this to teach, the whole world would listen.

TRANSFORMING LINES

Initial six: Viewing like a youth. This is not a mistake if you have nothing important to do. If you do, it means you have lost the Way.

Six at-second: Viewing by peeping through the screen like a woman. This can bring profit and insight, though you may see shameful things.

Six at-third: View your life and what you give birth to. Watch it advance and retreat. Then decide whether or not to act.

Six at-fourth: Viewing the shining of the city, invited to advise the king. Take advantage of your position. You are an honoured guest.

Nine at-fifth: View your life and what you give birth to. Then decide whether or not to act. This is not a mistake.

Nine above: View the lives and the origins of those around you. Then decide whether or not to act. This is not a mistake. Your purpose is not yet in order.

21 GNAWING AND BITING THROUGH, SHIH HO
Keywords: Confront the problem. Bite through the obstacle.

Gnawing and Biting Through shows how to confront a tenacious obstacle. Gnaw away at the obstacles then bite through what keeps things apart. The spirits will give you success, power and maturity. Going to court brings profit and insight.

Gnaw, Shih: Bite away, chew through; arrive at, attain; reach the truth by removing the nonessential. The ideogram suggests finding the truth by divination.

Bite, Ho: Unite, bring together; close the jaws, crush, chew; the sound of voices. The ideogram shows the jaws coming together.

The hexagram shows inner determination breaking through obstacles. Thunder and lightning. Take resolute action. Provide what is needed. Early kings used this to clarify punishments and enforce the laws. Gnaw and bite through! The spirits will give you success, power and maturity. Stir things up. Unite the shock of thunder and the clarity of lightning. Bringing things to judgement brings profit and insight.

ABOVE THIS HEXAGRAM MAY BE LINKED WITH THE LAW AND PUNISHMENTS.

TRANSFORMING LINES

Initial nine: Locked in the stocks, your feet disappear. This keeps you from moving for now. It is not a mistake.

Six at-second: Gnawing through flesh, your nose disappears. This enthusiasm is not a mistake. Don't be afraid to lose face. You are riding a solid force.

Six at-third: Gnawing through dried meat, you encounter poison. Don't simply let it go. You will lose the right way. This is not a mistake.

Nine at-fourth: Gnawing through meat parched on the bone. You acquire the ability to give things form and to direct your strength. Accepting drudgery and difficulty brings profit and insight. The Way is open. Things aren't clear yet, so keep on working.

Six at-fifth: Gnawing through parched meat. You acquire wealth and establish a line of descent. You are facing an angry old ghost. Go through the difficult time. This is not a mistake. You acquire what you need.

Nine above: Why are you putting your head in the stocks? Your ears disappear and you can't hear anything. This closes the Way. You certainly won't be enlightened like this.

22 ADORNING, PI
Keywords: Beautify things and be brave.

Adorning shows improving outward appearance. Beautify the way things are presented. Be elegant. Display your valour. The spirits will give you success, power and maturity. Adapt to what needs to be done. Having a direction brings profit and insight.

Adorn, Pi: Embellish, beautify; elegant, brilliant; inner worth seen in outer appearance; brave, eager, intrepid. The ideogram suggests linking worth and beauty.

The figure shows an outer limit producing radiant display. Fire beneath the mountain. Release bound energy. Things must be embellished to be seen. Brighten how you present yourself. Don't cut off processes already underway. The spirits give you success, power and maturity. Having a direction brings profit and insight. It reveals heaven's

RIGHT THE 22ND DIVINATORY FIGURE IS CONNECTED WITH BEAUTY, ADORNMENT AND EMBELLISHMENT.

design. Brightening the pattern and stopping there reveals it to the people. Look at the change the seasons bring. Use it to accomplish things.

TRANSFORMING LINES

Initial nine: Adorn your feet. Put aside your chariot and walk. Go your own way. This is the right thing to do.

Six at-second: Adorn your beard. Be brave and be patient. The connection with a superior is already there.

Nine at-third: Adorn yourself with this idea. Let it impregnate you. It will continually open the Way and provide for those who come after you.

Six at-fourth: Adorn this with the respect due to the old and venerable. It is like a soaring white horse that manifests creative energy. Whatever is approaching is not out to harm you. Make alliances. Bring things to completion.

Six at-fifth: While adorning the hilltop tombs, you realize the roll of silk you offer is very small. Don't despair. Going through with this opens the Way. It gives you cause to rejoice.

Nine above: Adorn this in white, what is clear, plain and pure. This is not a mistake. You will acquire a noble purpose.

23 STRIPPING, PO
Keywords: Strip away old ideas and habits.

Stripping shows getting rid of outmoded ideas. Strip away what has become unusable. Remove and uncover things. Cut into the problem without thought of immediate gain. Only then will having a direction bring profit and insight.

Strip, Po: Flay, peel, skin, scrape; remove, uncover, take off; diminish, reduce to essentials; prune trees, slaughter animals. The ideogram suggests taking decisive action to cut something away.

The hexagram shows the end of a cycle and preparation for the new. The mountain rests on earth. Re-establish creative balance by stripping away outmoded embellishments. There is something rotten here. Take action. Give generously to what is below to stabilize your position. Stripping away the old implies someone to carry it out. What is flexible and adaptable transforms what is solid and firm. Those who adapt will endure. Concentrate on the symbolic value of things, their power to connect you with the world of the spirits. Dissolve old structures so new action can emerge in the empty, fertile inner space. Heaven is moving there.

TRANSFORMING LINES

Initial six: Strip the bed, your resting place. Change your stand on things. If you ignore this, the Way will close.

Six at-second: Strip the bed, your resting place. Set yourself off from others. Bite into the matter at hand. If you ignore this, the Way will close. You don't have the proper associates yet.

Six at-third: Strip it away! This is not a mistake. Let it go.

Six at-fourth: If you try to strip your resting place this way, you will wound yourself and others. Don't do it. The Way will close. You are slicing close to calamity.

Six at-fifth: String the fish together. Profit and fertility are hidden in the stream of changing events. The palace ladies confer their grace and favour. Honour them. Use your connections and trust your imagination. There is nothing this will not benefit.

Nine above: There is a ripe fruit not eaten. Carry it away. If you simply adapt, your shelter will be stripped away. You cannot accomplish anything by staying where you are.

24 RETURNING, FU
Keywords: Go back and welcome the new beginning.

Returning shows re-emergence and re-birth. Go back to meet the returning energy and begin anew. Retrace your path, return to the source, restore the way. The spirits will give you success, power and maturity. Let things emerge and come back without pressure. People suggest mutual projects. It is not a mistake to join them. Turn and move away from your former path. The Way returns on the seventh day. Having a direction brings profit and insight.

Return, Fu: Go back, turn back, return to the start; come back, reappear; resurgence, re-birth, re-establish, renew, restore; an earlier time and place; beginning of the new time. The ideogram shows retracing a path.

The hexagram shows inner energy returning. Thunder in the earth. The old situation has been stripped away. Go to meet what is re-emerging. This is the root of realizing the Way. Be adaptable and differentiate yourself from others. Use your knowledge of the source. To nurture returning energy, Early kings closed the frontiers at the solstice. Merchants would not move about. The prince would not inspect the borders. The spirits will give you success, power and maturity. Stir things up. Let them emerge without pressure.

Join people in mutually profitable projects. Turn away from your former path. The Way returns on the seventh day. Heaven is moving here. Have a direction. The strong and firm will endure. By returning you see the heart of heaven and earth.

TRANSFORMING LINES

Initial nine: Don't put off returning. Don't simply repent. The Way is open. This renovates your whole being.

Six at-second: Return through letting go of what you are doing. The Way is open. Be unselfish and benevolent. Recognize your common humanity.

Six at-third: Urgent return, a critical moment. You are confronting an angry old ghost. Going through this difficult time is not a mistake.

Six at-fourth: Move to the centre. Return alone. The Way is open.

Six at-fifth: Generosity and wealth return. You will have no cause to regret this. The old wise men are behind you.

Six above: Delusion returns. The Way closes. If you act on this, you will incur disaster from within and without. Your forces will be completely ruined, their leader cut off and destroyed. It will take ten years to bring this disaster under control. Think about where this terrible desire comes from.

25 WITHOUT EMBROILING, WU WANG

Keywords: Disentangle yourself, then trust your intuition.

Without Embroiling shows how to act spontaneously. Free yourself from disorder. Disentangle yourself from compulsive ideas and emotions. This opens up a whole new cycle of time. If you do not correct yourself, you will always make mistakes through ignorance and delusion. Having a direction will bring no advantage.

Without, Wu: Devoid of, not having.

Embroiling, Wang: Caught up in, entangled, enmeshed; vain, rash, reckless, foolish, wild; lie, deceive; futile, false; brutal, insane, disordered.

The hexagram shows actions inspired by the spirit above. Thunder moves below heaven. If you return to the spirit, you will not be the source of disaster. Don't be caught in other people's disorder. Early kings used this to nourish the myriad beings. Firmness and strength from the outside activate a central principle. Respond to it. It links you with the spirits. By continually correcting yourself, you begin a period of power and enjoyment. Heaven will bestow it as fate. If not, you will consistently make mistakes and having a direction will bring no advantage. Without accord with the spirits, how can you do anything right? Heaven will not protect you. Disentangle yourself. Do it now!

TRANSFORMING LINES

Initial nine: Don't get entangled. Let the present situation go. This opens the Way. You acquire a new purpose.

Six at-second: Don't cultivate this crop, don't clear this land. This is not the right place to make an effort. If you realize this, having a direction brings profit and insight.

Six at-third: This isn't your fault. Stay unentangled. Perhaps there was an ox tied to a post belonging to a city person. If a traveller took the ox, the city dweller would think it a disaster. The traveller would acquire a new ox. Take your pick. Stay or move.

Nine at-fourth: An enabling divination. Put your ideas to the trial. This is not a mistake. It does no one harm.

Nine at-fifth: The disorder you are facing is not your fault. Don't attack it literally and you will soon have cause to rejoice.

Nine above: Stay unentangled. To act is a mistake. Do not have a direction. If you act, you will simply exhaust yourself and bring on disaster.

26 GREAT ACCUMULATING, TA CH'U
Keywords: Concentrate, focus, be active.

Great Accumulating shows a central idea that defines what is valuable. Focus on it to impose a direction on life. Concentrate on this goal. Gather all your many encounters. Think of yourself as raising animals, growing crops or bringing up children. Tolerate and nourish things. Putting your ideas to the trial brings profit and insight. It can culminate in great abundance. Don't stay at home. Be active. The Way is open. Enter the stream of life with a purpose

Great, Ta: Big, noble, important; able to protect others; a self-imposed goal; the ability to lead your life; yang energy.

Accumulate, Ch'u: Gather, collect, hoard, retain; control, restrain; take care of, support, tolerate; tame, pasture animals; raise children. The ideogram shows the fertile soil of a river delta.

RIGHT TA CH'U DEALS WITH ABUNDANCE, SYMBOLIZED
BY THE RAISING OF PASTURE ANIMALS.

The hexagram shows creative force accumulating within. Heaven in the centre of the mountain. You can realize your hidden potential. Put your purpose in order. Assimilate the records of your predecessors. Be firm, persist. Renew your power and your connection to the Way each day. Honour moral and intellectual power. Don't stay at home. Taking in what comes opens the Way. Step into the stream of life with a purpose. The connections reach to heaven.

TRANSFORMING LINES

Initial nine: This situation is possessed by an angry old ghost. Decline the challenge and get out of the way of disaster. That brings profit and insight.

Nine at-second: The cart is stopped by the axle-straps. Relationships have broken down and you can't carry on. Stay in the centre and don't try to compete.

Nine at-third: Mounted on a fine horse, in pursuit of your goals. If you can accept drudgery, put your ideas to the trial. Imagine it like this: you are escorting a precious hidden cargo. Having a direction brings profit and insight.

Six at-fourth: Collect young cattle in a stable. Accumulate the strength to carry heavy loads and confront difficult situations. This opens the Way to the Source. It will give you cause to rejoice.

Six at-fifth: The tusks of a gelded boar. An old enemy can't do you harm. The Way is open. This brings you rewards.

Nine above: Isn't this the road of the heavenly spirits? Your idea pleases them. They will give you success, effective power and the capacity to bring things to maturity. The Way is moving in your idea. This begins a flourishing and productive time.

27 THE JAWS/SWALLOWING, YI
Keywords: Take in what has happened. Provide nourishment.

Jaws/Swallowing shows what goes in and out of the mouth. Provide for yourself and others. Take in what has been done and let it nourish the new. Feed yourself and your dependants. The way is open. Seek the source of nourishment. The answer to your question lies there.

Jaws/Swallowing, Yi: Mouth, jaws; eat, take in; feed, nourish, sustain, bring up; provide what is necessary. The ideogram shows an open mouth.

The hexagram shows accomplishments being swallowed to nourish new growth. Thunder within the mountain. Correct the way things are nourished. Consider your words carefully. Articulate how you eat and drink. The Way is open. Look at where and how things are nourished. Heaven and earth nourish the myriad beings. The sages nourish what is excellent. This is truly a time to be great.

TRANSFORMING LINES
Initial nine: You set your soul-tortoise aside and contemplate your sagging jaws. You have let go of your magic. No wonder you look so sad. This has no value whatsoever. The Way closes.

Six at-second: Your connection to nourishment is toppling. Reject the rules. Go to your graves and shrines to think this over. Trying to put others in order will simply close the Way.

Six at-third: You are rejecting what nourishes you. The Way closes. If you go on like this, you won't be able to act for ten years. This is not advantageous. Your idea goes against the Way.

63

Six at-fourth: Your connection to nourishment is toppling. Find a new one. The Way is open. Be like a tiger. When you look, look hard. When you desire, pursue it. This zeal is not a mistake. You brighten things through your efforts.

Six at-fifth: Reject the rules. Stay where you are and put your ideas to the trial. The Way is open. Don't enter the stream of life with a goal for now. Yield to the impulse that comes from above.

Nine above: Nourished by what has come before you, you must confront an angry old ghost. Going through the difficulties opens the Way. Enter the stream of events with a purpose. Your idea will be rewarded.

28 GREAT EXCEEDING, TA KUO
Keywords: A crisis. Gather all your force. Don't be afraid to act alone.

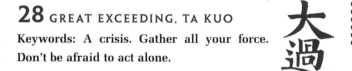

Great Exceeding shows how to act in a time of crisis. Push your principles beyond ordinary limits. Have a noble purpose. Find what is truly important and organize yourself. The ridgepole of the house is sagging. The structure of your life is in danger of collapse. But there is a creative force at work in this breakdown. Have a direction. The spirits will give you success, power and maturity.

Great, Ta: Big, noble, important; able to protect others; a self-imposed goal; the ability to lead your life; yang energy.

Exceed, Ku: Go beyond, surpass, overtake, overshoot; get clear of, get over; cross the threshold, surmount difficulties; transgress the norms, outside the limits.

The hexagram shows outer events overwhelming inner penetration. Mists submerge the trees. There is a creative force at work in this breakdown. If your situation doesn't nourish you, push it over and leave. Don't be afraid to go it alone. Don't be sad about retiring from the community. Having a great idea means being excessive. The structure of your life is sagging. The places where you make contact are fading. Let the strong force gathering stimulate movement. Have a direction. The spirits will give you success, power and maturity. This is a very great time.

TRANSFORMING LINES

Initial six: Prepare carefully. Spread an offering mat. Be clear and concentrate on essentials. Great things have humble beginnings.

Nine at-second: A withered willow gives birth to new shoots. An old husband acquires a young bride. A burst of real new growth.

ABOVE THE TA KUO HEXAGRAM IS LINKED WITH NEW GROWTH.

65

Nine at-third: The ridgepole buckles, the structure fails. The Way is closed. There is no way to brace the situation up.

Nine at-fourth: The ridgepole is crowned. The structure is braced and strengthened. The Way opens. Don't try to go any further. Trying to add to this will only bring shame and confusion.

Nine at-fifth: A withered willow gives birth to flowers. An old wife acquires a young husband. A brief burst of beauty. There is neither praise nor blame. Enjoy it. It won't last long.

Six above: If you go beyond wading in this water, you may go under. The Way will close through no fault of your own. Choose carefully how far you want to involve yourself. It reflects on something bigger than everyday concerns.

29 REPEATING GORGE/ VENTURING, HSI K'AN

Keywords: Collect your forces. Take the risk. Do it again and again.

坎

Repeating Gorge shows how to confront something dangerous and difficult. You must take the risk without holding back. You cannot avoid this obstacle. Be like water that falls, fills up a hole and flows on. Practise, train, accustom yourself to danger. This is a critical point. Attention! It could become a grave. Summon your energy. Confront the challenge. You are linked to the spirits and they will carry you through. Hold fast to your heart. The spirits will give you success, power and maturity. Taking action now brings honour.

Repeat, Hsi: Practise, rehearse, train; familiar with, skilled; repeat a lesson. The ideogram shows a winged cap, thought carried forward by repeated movement.

Gorge, K'an: A dangerous place; hole, cavity, pit, steep precipice; snare, trap, grave; a critical time, a test; take risks without reserve. The ideogram shows a deep hole into which water flows.

ABOVE THIS HEXAGRAM SUGGESTS DANGER, PARTICULARLY OF SNARES OR OF BEING TRAPPED.

The hexagram shows water repeatedly flowing into the gorge. Repeating streams reach the goal. Overflowing energy is moving toward the depths. Act on your principles. When you teach and when you act, repeat things again and again. Redouble your efforts. Gather your desires and hold on to your heart's growth. Moving and acting now will bring honour. Gorge means danger. A danger confronted and used is an accomplishment and a defence. Concentrate your forces and take risks.

TRANSFORMING LINES

Initial six: Repeating the gorge, you are caught in the pit, a fatal diversion. This is a habitual mistake. The Way closes.

Nine at-second: A difficult passage. Take the risk. Seek out what you need. You will acquire it by being flexible and adaptable.

Six at-third: Gorge after gorge is coming at you. If you take action now, you will be trapped in a fatal diversion. You won't achieve anything. Are you sure you know what you want?

Six at-fourth: Trapped in the gorge. Lay out a meal for the spirits. Offer a cup with liquor, the distillation of your efforts. Set out two clay vessels, the symbols of your heart and body. Open yourself and the spirit will come through the window to give you what you need. It will set you free.

Nine at-fifth: Not too much effort. The water is already rising. This is not a mistake. Stay in the centre. Don't make a great fuss.

Six above: Bound with ropes and sent off to the thorn bushes to be judged and found wanting. If you go on like this, you won't get anywhere for three years. The Way is closed.

30 RADIANCE/CLARIFYING, LI
Keywords: Articulate and spread the light and warmth.

Radiance shows growing awareness. Spread the light and warmth. This is a time of intelligent effort. It includes unexpected encounters and extraordinary experiences. Put your ideas to the trial. The spirits will give you power, enjoyment and maturity. Accumulate the receptive strength that can carry burdens. The Way is open.

Radiance, Li: Light, warmth and fire; illuminate, discriminate, articulate, arrange; consciousness, awareness; separate yourself from, step outside the norms, encounter by chance; adhere to, depend on. The ideogram shows a magical bird with brilliant plumage.

LEFT THE 30TH HEXAGRAM IS CONNECTED WITH FIRE AND WARMTH.

The hexagram shows awareness enduring and spreading. Brightness doubled arouses Radiance. Concentrate your energy. Bring things together. Radiance is shining above. Use it again and again to spread clarity to the four corners of the world. Radiance connects and illuminates things. The sun and moon illuminate heaven. The grains, grasses and trees illuminate the earth. Brightening things reinforces correcting. This is how change occurs. Be flexible and adaptable. It is pleasing to the spirits. Accumulating the receptive strength that can carry burdens opens the Way.

Transforming Lines

Initial nine: Polish the beginning. Proceed step by step. Respect things. Inquire into motives. Then you won't make a mistake.

Six at-second: Yellow radiance, light from the earth. This opens the Way to the Source. You acquire the centre and connect with the Way.

Nine at-third: You are seeing things in the light of the setting sun. Instead of beating your drums and singing your songs, you sit there like a very old person lamenting all the terrible things that have happened. This closes the Way. Why go on like this?

Nine at-fourth: This comes on like a sudden assault. It burns up, dies and you can throw it away. It doesn't have a place in your life.

Six at-fifth: Cry over this as if your sorrow would never end. This opens the Way. You feel you have lost your central relationship, but the connection is still there underneath it all.

Nine above: The king sends out troops to punish the rebels. This is an excellent thing to do. Sever the head, the centre of the opposition, and let the smaller demons go. The opposition will fall apart. The Way is open. You can correct the order of things.

31 CONJOINING, HSIEN
Keywords: Be open to the influence. Bring things together.

Conjoining shows an influence that triggers action and unites what belongs together. Reach out, join things, allow yourself to be moved. This brings profit and insight. The spirits will give you success, power and maturity. Understanding and embracing the woman and the yin opens the Way.

69

Conjoin, Hsien: Contact, influence, move; excite, mobilize, trigger; all, entire; unite, bring together the parts of a separated whole; conjunction, as the planets; literally: broken piece of pottery, the halves of which were joined to identify partners.

The hexagram figure shows inner strength submitting to outer stimulation. The mists above the mountain. This reflects the way the world is made. When heaven and earth conjoin, the myriad beings appear. Man and woman become husband and wife, chief and servant order what is above and

RIGHT THIS HEXAGRAM GOVERNS UNITY
AND BRINGING THINGS TOGETHER.

below and individuals have a way to order their hearts. Bring people together through accepting them. You can move the hearts of others. Accept and embrace the woman and the yin. The spirits will give you success, power, profit and insight. When heaven and earth influence each other, the myriad beings change and give birth. When the sage influences people's hearts, the world is harmonized. Contemplate how people can be touched and you can move the heart of heaven, earth and the myriad beings.

TRANSFORMING LINES

Initial six: This impulse stimulates your big toes. It comes from far and is in its beginning. Locate your purpose outside yourself.

Six at-second: The impulse stimulates your calves. Staying where you are opens the Way. If you run after it, you will fall into a pit. The Way will close. Yield and stay free of harm.

Nine at-third: This impulse stimulates your thighs. Hold on to your desire to follow or the Way will close. This will not last. Stay where you are and find your purpose in those who follow you. Hold on to what is below.

Nine at-fourth: Take action. This opens the Way. All cause for regret will be extinguished. The impulse wavers, so you may be indecisive. Simply think about it deeply and the help you need will arrive.

Nine at-fifth: The impulse stimulates your spine, neck and shoulders. This deep connection brings no cause for regrets. It will manifest over time. Yielding to this will bring no cause for regret.

Six above: The impulse stimulates your jaws, cheeks and tongue, so you produce a torrent of stimulating words. This energy won't last long, so be ready to pull back when it ends.

32 PERSEVERING, HENG
**Keywords: Continue on.
Renew your efforts.**

Persevering shows what continues and endures. Keep on the way you are going. Persist in your way of life and what you feel is right. The spirits will give you success, power and maturity. This is not a mistake. Having a direction brings profit and insight.

Persevere, Heng: Continue in the same way or spirit; constant, stable, regular; enduring, durable, permanent, self-renewing; ordinary, habitual; extend everywhere; the moon when it is almost full. The ideogram suggests enduring in the voyage of life.

The hexagram figure shows arousing energy coupled with inner penetration. Thunder and wind. The way of the husband and wife. Persevering steadies the power to realize the Way. This is a time for resolute action. Establish principles and boundaries that endure. Thunder and wind work together to ground things and stir up new growth. What is solid and what is supple are in harmony. Endure in the way of heaven and earth. When you complete something, let it become the beginning of the new. The sun and the moon have heaven, and thus their light endures. The four seasons endure and transform and they enable lasting accomplishment. The wise person endures in the Way and the human world perfects itself. Contemplate how things persevere and you see the purpose of the myriad beings.

TRANSFORMING LINES

Initial six: Deepening through persevering, too deep, too soon. The Way closes. There is nothing you can do that would be advantageous.

Nine at-second: Take action. All your regrets will be extinguished. This brings lasting ability, power and skill.

Nine at-third: Not persevering in the power to realize the Way. If you receive gifts, you will only be embarrassed. The Way closes. There is nothing that can help you here.

Nine at-fourth: No game in these fields. Do not persevere in this situation! Slip away quietly and acquire what you need.

Six at-fifth: Choose how you will persevere. If you want to act like a wife, continuing on will open the Way. Adhere to this one thing and follow it through. If you want to act like a husband or a son, continuing on closes the Way. Cut yourself off from this situation to preserve your integrity.

Six above: Rousing persevering. Too much agitation. If you go on like this, the Way will close. If a commander acts like this, nothing will be achieved.

72

33 RETIRING, TUN

Keywords: **Withdraw, conceal yourself, be small, be happy.**

Retiring shows withdrawal in the face of conflict. Pull back and seclude yourself to prepare for a better time. This brings profit and insight. The spirits will give you success, power and maturity. Don't impose your ideas. Adapt to whatever crosses your path.

Retire, Tun: Withdraw, run away, escape, hide yourself; disappear, withdraw into obscurity, become invisible; secluded, anti-social; fool or trick someone. The ideogram suggests satisfaction, luck and wealth through withdrawing.

The hexagram shows an inner limit that connects with spirit above. Below heaven, the mountain. You can't stay where you are. Withdraw, pull back, decline involvements, refuse connections. Keep people at a distance through a demanding severity that inspires fear and awe. Retiring is pleasing to the spirits. It corresponds to the movement of the time. Be adaptable and flexible. Immerse yourself in the situation and endure. Knowing when to retire is a great and righteous thing!

TRANSFORMING LINES

Initial six: Retiring's tail. You are caught and held fast. You confront an angry old ghost. It is no use to have a direction. Stay where you are for now and avoid calamity.

Six at-second: Bind yourself to this. Don't let anything pry you loose. Make your purpose firm, then move with it out of danger.

Nine at-third: Tied retiring. You confront an angry ghost. You can't do this alone. Gather servants, who can communicate with the authorities, and concubines, who can create a pleasing atmosphere. This is an exhausting task. You will not be able to achieve anything great for now. Content yourself with getting free.

Nine at-fourth: Pleasurable retiring opens the Way. Use the oracle to stay in touch with the Way. Don't be adaptable. Don't talk to unimportant people.

Nine at-fifth: Excellence through retiring. This opens the Way. Your purpose is correct. Don't doubt yourself.

Nine above: Fertile retiring. There is nothing this will not benefit. It ushers in a time of abundance.

34 GREAT INVIGORATING, TA CHUANG

Keywords: Have a firm purpose. Focus your strength and go forward.

Great Invigorating shows strength, drive and invigorating power. Focus your strength through a creative idea and go forward. This brings profit and insight. Don't hurt others through excessive force.

Great, Ta: Big, noble, important; able to protect others; a self-imposed goal; the ability to lead your life; yang energy.

Invigorate, Chuang: Inspire, animate, strengthen; strong, flourishing, robust; mature, in the prime of life; also: damage, wound, unrestrained use of strength. The ideogram shows a man stout and strong as a tree.

The hexagram shows inner force expressed directly. Thunder above heaven. Come out of retirement. Hold on to your strength and proceed on your own. A great idea implies power. Correct one-sidedness in yourself and others. Having a great idea and correcting your path lets you see the heart of heaven and earth.

74

Transforming Lines

Initial nine: Invigorating in your feet. Hold back for now. If you set out on an expedition or discipline people, the Way will close. You are linked to the spirits and they will carry you through. There is the danger of exhaustion if you act too quickly.

Nine at-second: The Way is open. Put your plan to the trial.

Nine at-third: Only small people use force. Be empty. Use a net, not a club. You are confronting an angry old ghost. If you charge ahead like a ram butting a hedge, you will entangle your horns and lose your power.

Nine at-fourth: The Way is open. The obstacle breaks up. Use your strength like a great cart. Bring things together and carry them forward. Now is the time to accomplish things.

Six at-fifth: You lose your sheep, but be versatile. Move with the change. You will have no cause to regret it. Your current situation is not appropriate.

Six above: A ram butts a hedge. He can't pull back, and he can't break through. You are caught and are in for a spell of drudgery. This will open the Way. A lack of forethought got you stuck, but the fault won't last long.

35 PROSPERING, CHIN
Keywords: Step into the light. Give and receive gifts. Welcome the new day.

Prospering shows emerging into the full light of day. Be calm in your strength and poise. Take delight in things. Give strength and spirit to enhance those connected with you. You will be received by higher powers three times in a day.

Prosper, Chin: Grow and flourish, as young plants do in the sun; advance, increase, progress; be promoted, rise; permeate, impregnate. The ideogram shows birds taking flight at dawn.

The hexagram shows emerging light. Brightness issues forth above earth. Prospering is a time to advance. Yield and join with others to brighten your own great idea. What is flexible and adaptable will move you to the position above. Be calm in your strength and poise and give gifts of strength and spirit. You will be received by the higher powers three times in one day.

TRANSFORMING LINES
Initial six: In order to prosper, hold back at first. The Way is open. But use a net, not a club. You are linked to the spirits and they will carry you through. Be generous and take independent action to correct the situation. You have not yet received your mandate from fate.

Six at-second: In order to prosper, accept this sorrow the situation brings. The Way is open. This is a constricting situation, but it brings great blessing from the queen and the mothers.

Six at-third: The crowds have confidence in you. All cause to repent is extinguished. People affirm you. Move upwards.

Nine at-fourth: Prosperity brings bushy-tailed rodents, timid skulking animals that steal and eat up stored grain. You confront an angry old ghost. Don't act now. The situation is not appropriate.

Six at-fifth: Take action. All cause to repent will be extinguished. Don't worry about gain or loss. Have no cares, the Way is open. There is nothing this will not benefit. To go on brings rewards.

Nine above: Use your strength carefully. Confronting your own ghosts opens the Way. This is not a mistake. Your path is not clear yet.

36 BRIGHTNESS HIDING, MING YI
Keywords: Hide your light. Accept the difficult task.

Brightness Hiding shows entering the darkness. Conceal your intelligence by entering what is beneath you. There is a real possibility of injury here. By dimming your light you avoid it. Accepting drudgery will bring you profit and insight.

Brightness, Ming: Fire, sun, moon and stars; consciousness, awareness, intelligence; illuminate, distinguish; lucid, clear. The ideogram shows the sun and the moon.

Hide, Yi: Keep out of sight; distant, remote; raze, level; ordinary, colourless; cut, wound, destroy; barbarians, vulgar, uncultured people. The ideogram shows a threatening man with a bow.

The hexagram shows inner light hidden in common labour. Brightness enters the earth's centre. Accept what is confronting you. You are being proscribed and excluded. Watch the desires that connect you with others. Choose when to darken or to brighten them. Brighten the pattern within yourself. Use the obscurity to clarify worthy ideas, like King Wen, who organized the *I Ching* when he was imprisoned by a tyrant. Accept the heaviness like Prince Chi, who distinguished what is right in a difficult time and became a model for others.

TRANSFORMING LINES

Initial nine: Hide your brightness through flying. Though your wings droop, carry on for three days without eating. Have a direction. If you can master your words in this dangerous situation, you will persuade others of your authority.

Six at-second: Hiding your brightness, you are wounded in the left thigh. This is a serious but not deadly wound. Use the strength of a horse and come to the rescue! The Way is open.

Nine at-third: Hiding your brightness in the southern hunt. You capture the great leader. In time, this will free you from affliction.

Six at-fourth: You enter the left belly and take the heart of the hiding brightness. Leave this place, this family, this way of thinking. You have captured the meaning, so don't be sorry. Get out now!

Six at-fifth: Hide your brightness like Prince Chi, who went on in a difficult time without losing his integrity. Don't pause in your efforts to clarify things.

Nine above: At first he mounts to heaven, then he falls to earth. This is the position of the oppressive tyrant who falls at last. The dark time is over.

37 DWELLING (CLAN) PEOPLE, CHIA JEN

Keywords: Hold together. Stay inside. Adapt, nourish, endure.

Dwelling People shows living and working with others. Care for the people who share your space and your activities. Profit and insight come through the woman and a nourishing attitude. Dwell in the yin.

Dwell, Chi: Home, household, family, relations, clan; a school of thought; master of a skill; hold something in common. The ideogram shows valued domestic animals.

LEFT THE 37TH HEXAGRAM IS ASSOCIATED WITH HOUSEHOLDS AND FAMILIES.

People, Jen: Human beings; an individual; humanity. The ideogram shows a person kneeling.

The hexagram shows warmth and clarity spreading from within. Wind originating from fire issues forth. When you are injured in the outer world, you turn back to the dwelling. Dwelling people means what is inside. Use your words to connect with people and make your actions persevering. A woman's attitude corrects the situation inside; a man's attitude corrects the situation

RIGHT THIS FIGURE MAY SUGGEST TAKING SHELTER.

outside. Together they reflect the righteousness of heaven and earth. When you correct the dwelling, you set the world right.

TRANSFORMING LINES

Initial nine: Fences are what define a dwelling. Stay inside it now, and your regrets will disappear. Your purpose hasn't transformed itself yet. Define your boundaries and feel secure within them.

Six at-second: Respond to what needs to be done. Dwell in the inner centre. Prepare the meals and the offerings. The Way is open.

Nine at-third: Repenting past adversity and severity opens the Way. But if the wife and child laugh at this, it closes the Way. Without a structure, the dwelling will simply dissolve. Impose limits.

Six at-fourth: This is an affluent dwelling. The Way is open. Your central idea can help and nourish others.

Nine at-fifth: A king imagines this dwelling. Have no cares and act from your heart. This generates meaning and good fortune. The Way is open. Mingle with others in mutual affection.

Nine above: You are linked to the spirits and they will carry you through. You impress everyone through this power. Completing your plan opens the Way. You have the spirits behind you.

38 DIVERGING, K'UEI
Keywords: Change conflict into creative tension through awareness.

Diverging shows opposition and discord. You must separate and clarify what is in conflict while acknowledging the essential connection. Being flexible and adaptable opens the Way. Be open to strange occurrences and sudden visions.

Diverge, Kuei: Oppose, separate, distant; at odds, discordant, antagonistic, contrary, exclusive; astronomical or polar opposition; look at things from an unusual perspective.

The hexagram shows expression and awareness in conflict with each other. Fire rises, the mists descend. When the way of dwelling together is exhausted, you must turn away. Diverging is what is outside. Learn to both join things and to separate them. Fire and mists are like two women who live together while their purposes move apart. They can be connected through brightness and awareness. Use what is flexible and adaptable. This opens the Way. Heaven and earth diverge, but they work together. Man and woman diverge, but their purposes connect. The myriad beings diverge, but all are busy with the same things. Examine what separates and what connects people. You can connect with what is truly great.

Transforming Lines

Initial nine: Even though you have lost your horse, don't pursue it. It will return by itself. When you see hateful people, don't get entangled in their twisted emotions.

Nine at-second: You meet a lord in a narrow street, someone important who can help and teach you. The meeting is not a mistake. You have not let go of the Way.

Six at-third: You see a cart being dragged back, the cattle hobbled, the people's heads shaved and noses cut off. All lose face and honour. You will not be able to carry your plan to completion. The situation is not appropriate.

Nine at-fourth: You are alone, like an orphan without a protector. You will unexpectedly meet a powerful being, a source of good fortune and benevolent care. Join this being with confidence. The spirits are with you and will carry you through. This is not a mistake.

Six at-fifth: Your regrets will disappear. Your ancestor gnaws through the obstacles to find you. You are linked with friends and ancestral spirits. How could this be a mistake?

Nine above: You are alone, like an orphan without a protector. You see strange visions of pigs carrying mud on their backs, a chariot full of ghosts. Is this what you think of the people around you? Collect yourself! At first you draw the bow against attack, then you unbend it in friendship. Seek alliances and marriages. As you go on, you will meet the cleansing rain. The Way is open.

39 DIFFICULTIES, CHIEN
Keywords: Don't act. Re-imagine the situation.

Difficulties show obstacles and the feeling of affliction. You must see through the situation in a new way and gather energy for a decisive new move. Join with others in view of future gains. Lonely efforts and dwelling on the past won't help. Great people can help you think about the situation. The Way is open.

Difficulties, Chien: Walk lamely, proceed haltingly; difficulties, obstacles, obstructions; the feeling of being afflicted, unhappy, suffering; crooked, feeble; poverty; pride. The ideogram shows cold feet and bad circulation.

The hexagram shows an inner limit and outer danger. Mountain above the gorge. Turning away is always arduous. But by reversing your direction, you can renovate your power. This is a difficult and heavy time. There is danger in front of you; if you can see it and stop, you will really understand the situation. Retreating and joining with others brings profit and insight. Attack and lonely striving will close the Way. Consult those who can help you to see what is great. This leads to achievement. The Way will open.

Correct how you use power and who you depend on. By re-imagining your situation, you connect with what is truly great.

Initial six: Difficulties are going, praise is coming. The proper thing to do is to wait for it.

Six at-second: A king's servant encounters difficulty after difficulty. He is in no way the source of the trouble. Don't doubt yourself. Bring things to completion as simply as you can.

Nine at-third: Difficulty is going, the reversal is coming. Stay inside. You will soon have cause to rejoice.

Six at-fourth: Difficulty is going, connections are coming. The new time has real value.

Nine at-fifth: In great difficulties, you meet friends and partners. Make articulating these connections the centre of your concerns.

Six above: Difficulty is going, eminence is coming. The time is ripe. The Way opens. Consult those who can help you to see what is great. Hold on to what you feel is valuable.

40 LOOSENING/DELIVERANCE, HSIEH

Keywords: Solve problems, untie knots, release blocked energy.

Loosening shows release from tension and the new energy that it brings. Untie knots, dispel sorrows, solve problems. Forgive and forget. Join with others to realize plans for future gain. If you have no unfinished business, simply wait for the energy to return. If you have things to do, be up at the crack of dawn. The Way is open.

Loosening/Deliverance, Hsieh: Divide, detach, untie, scatter, sever, dissolve; analyse, understand; free from constraint, dispel sorrow, eliminate effects, solve problems; get rid of; take care of needs. The ideogram shows a horn tool used to loosen knots.

The hexagram shows the fertile shock of a stirring new time. Thunder and rain arousing. Deliverance implies relaxing and letting things go. Forgive excesses, pardon faults. It means arousing things and avoiding danger. Act to stir things up. Join with others to realize plans for future gain. You will acquire the crowds. The returning energy opens the Way. If you have things to do, be up at dawn's first light. This brings achievement. Heaven and earth loosen and free things through the power of thunder and rain. Thunder and rain rouse the seeds of the fruits, grasses and trees to burst forth. The time of loosening is a great time indeed.

ABOVE THIS HEXAGRAM SUGGESTS LOOSENING TIES.

TRANSFORMING LINES

Initial six: Act on your plan. There is no harm in this. You are right at the border, the point of emergence.

Nine at-second: You catch three foxes and acquire a yellow arrow. This is an omen of power. Put your ideas to the trial. The Way is open.

Six at-third: Carrying a burden and riding in a coach. One way or another, you are not in your place. This will attract robbers and put you to shame. The fault lies with you. Get rid of it.

Nine at-fourth: Loosen your thumbs. Bring partnerships to an end and go on alone. You are connected to the spirits and they will carry you through. New connections are on the way.

Six at-fifth: You are held fast, but deliverance will come. Hold on to your purpose. The Way is open. You are connected to the spirits and they will carry you through. Adapt to what crosses your path. This lets you withdraw from the situation.

Six above: A prince shoots a hawk on the high rampart above. He catches it. There is nothing this will not benefit. It dissolves a perverse obstruction.

41 DIMINISHING, SUN

Keywords: Diminish yourself, decrease your involvements.

The hexagram Diminishing shows sacrifice, loss and developing inner concentration. Decrease your involvements and free yourself from emotional entanglements. You are connected to the spirits and they will carry you through. This opens the Way to the Source. It is not a mistake. Have a direction. Inquire into motivations. Use two ceremonial vessels to make an offering to the spirits.

Diminish, Sun: Lessen, take away, make smaller; weaken, humble; damage, lose, hurt; offer in sacrifice, give up, give away; concentrate, purify. The ideogram suggests making an offering.

The hexagram shows an outer limit that promotes inner development. Below the mountain, the mists. To

LEFT THE IDEOGRAM FOR THIS FIGURE SUGGESTS MIST BELOW MOUNTAINS.

release blocked energy, you must let things go. Decreasing is the beginning of increasing. This is the way you repair your virtue and power. It is arduous at first, but lets you change with the time. It keeps harm at a distance. Curb your anger; block your passions. Diminish what is below and augment what is above. You are connected to the spirits and they will carry you through. This opens the Way to the Source. Inquire into motivations. Use two ceremonial vessels. This means diminishing what is strong and augmenting what is supple in order to fill what is empty. It lets you move with the time.

TRANSFORMING LINES

Initial nine: Bring this to a close and leave quickly. This is not a mistake. Discuss what diminishing can bring. Have a noble purpose.

Nine at-second: Put your ideas to the trial. Don't discipline people or set out on an expedition. That closes the Way. Nothing will be diminished by this, everything will be augmented.

Six at-third: When three people move, they are diminished by one. When one person moves, a friend comes. Have no doubts.

Six at-fourth: Your affliction will be diminished by doing this. Send the message quickly. It is not a mistake. It is truly a cause for rejoicing.

Six at-fifth: Ten divinations with the tortoise shell oracle could not contradict this! The Way to the Source is open. The spirit above protects and shields its birth.

Nine above: Nothing will be diminished by this, everything will be augmented. This is not a mistake. The Way is open. Have a direction. You obtain people to help you but not a dwelling place. Your purpose makes great gains.

42 AUGMENTING, YI

Keywords: A fertile time.
Expand, increase, pour in more.

Augmenting shows advance and development. Increase your involvement and pour in more energy. This is a time of gain, profit and expansion. Have a direction. Enter the stream of life with a purpose. This brings profit and insight.

LEFT THIS HEXAGRAM IS ASSOCIATED WITH ABUNDANCE AND WEALTH.

Augment, Yi: Increase, advance, add to; benefit, strengthen, support; pour in more, overflowing; fertile, useful, profitable, advantageous. The ideogram shows a vessel overflowing with material and spiritual benefits.

The hexagram shows arousing new energy penetrating the world. Wind and thunder augmenting. By diminishing things, you have created augmenting, for increase and decrease are each other's beginning. Through augmenting you enrich your power and virtue and can enrich other things without limits. When you can imagine improvement, change. When there is excess, correct it. Diminish what is above and augment what is below. Stimulate people at their work. Have a direction. Correct one-sidedness and error. Entering the stream of life with a purpose brings profit and insight. Secure your vehicle then make your move. When heaven spreads out, earth gives birth. Together they augment things on all sides. This connects you with the time, so move with it.

TRANSFORMING LINES

Initial nine: Activate your ideas and rouse yourself to begin great efforts. This opens the Way to the Source. This is not a mistake, even though your resources are limited.

Six at-second: Ten divinations with the tortoise-shell oracle could not contradict your plan! It opens the Way to the Source. Be like the king presenting a sacrifice to the supreme powers. Use this to create good fortune for all. What augments you is indeed on its way.

Six at-third: Augmented though the Way is closed. This is not a mistake. You are connected to the spirits and they will carry you through. The centre is moving. Notify the authorities and connect the movement with your basic principles.

Six at-fourth: The centre of your life is moving. Notify the authorities and connect the movement with your basic principles. Actively involve yourself in this change and you augment your own purpose.

87

Nine at-fifth: You are connected to the spirits and they will carry you through. Act with a benevolent heart. This opens the Way to the Source. Benevolence is your personal key to power and virtue. Your purpose will make great gains.

Nine above: This augments nothing! It closes the Way. You have not given your heart an enduring foundation. If you go on like this, you will only attract disaster.

43 DECIDING, KUAI
Keywords: Decide and act resolutely. Clean it out and bring it to light.

Deciding shows how to confront difficulties. Clarify what you must do and act even if you must leave things behind. Announce your decision. You are connected to the spirits and they will carry you through. You are confronting an angry old ghost. Notify those who depend on you. Don't resort to arms. Having a direction brings profit and insight.

Deciding, Kuai: Decide, declare, resolve on; resolute, prompt, decisive, stern; certain, settled; open and cleanse a wound; water bursting through a barrier; separate, fork, flow in different directions.

The hexagram shows inner force coming to expression. The mists rise above heaven. Act with drive and persistence. By continually augmenting things you break through obstacles. Deciding means breaking up barriers. Spread your wealth to those below you. Persist in your efforts to express things. Break through the obstacles to harmony. Display your resolution in the centre of power. Strong forces are behind you. The spirits will give you the power. Exposure to danger will make you shine. Notify those who depend on you. Don't resort to arms. Have a direction. What is strong and solid endures. Bring your plan to completion.

TRANSFORMING LINES

Initial nine: Invigorating strength in the foot behind you. This is not the way to activate things. Your stance is faulty. If you proceed like this, you will fail.

Nine at-second: Alarms and outcries. Be on guard day and night. Have no cares, you will acquire what you want.

Nine at-third: There is invigorating strength in the cheekbones. These are cruel people who insist on their mastery. By associating with you will close the Way. Resolutely leave this situation. Going on alone, you will be caught in the rain, soaked and polluted. Your feeling of indignation at how you have been treated is not a mistake. Part from these people!

Nine at-fourth: Hurt, flayed or punished, you are moving on. You feel dragged like a goat on a leash. Don't lose your capacity to act. Your doubts and regrets will soon vanish. Don't trust what people tell you. Your understanding will not be brightened by this talk.

Nine at-fifth: A bunch of proliferating weeds calls for resolute action. Get to the centre and pull it up. This is not a mistake. Your purpose is hidden by the swampy growth.

Six above: Don't go on without communicating. It closes the Way. Call out! Communicate! Tell us about it!

44 COUPLING/WELCOMING, KOU
**Keywords: Welcome it, then let it go.
Trust what the experience brings.**

Welcoming shows opening to what comes. This encounter connects the primal powers. Don't try to control it. The woman and the yin are full of strength. Embrace the woman. This connects you with a creative force.

Coupling/Welcoming, Kou: Encounter, meet on your path; copulate, all forms of sexual intercourse; yin and yang, magnetism, gravity, mating of animals; be gripped by impersonal forces; favourable, enjoyable. The ideogram portrays sexual intercourse.

The hexagram shows spirit spreading in the world. Below heaven there is wind. It implies unexpected encounters, lucky coincidences, enjoyable happenings. Queens and kings use this to spread their

RIGHT THE KOU HEXAGRAM IS CONNECTED WITH THE UNION OF MALE
AND FEMALE, SYMBOLIZED HERE BY THE SIGNS FOR MARS AND VENUS.

mandates to the four corners of the world. Don't grasp and hold on to things. Although these contacts can't endure, heaven and earth meet and all the beings join in beautiful display. The time of welcoming is truly and righteously great!

TRANSFORMING LINES

Initial six: Attached to a metal chock. Movement stops. This opens the Way. Find a direction. See how you are trapped. Something is interfering with the flow of wealth, good fortune and enjoyment. Find out why this emaciated pig is dragging its lame hoof. It will connect you to the spirits and carry you through.

Nine at-second: There are fish in this enclosure, a womb pregnant with abundance. This is not a mistake. Don't invite guests and don't visit others. Don't extend yourself.

Nine at-third: Hurt or punished, you are moving on. You confront an angry old ghost. Danger. If you can find a central idea, you will make no great mistake. Don't simply be dragged along.

Nine at-fourth: This enclosure has no fish; a sterile womb. Don't try to undertake anything. The Way is closed.

Nine at-fifth: Weaving willow branches to enclose melons, a symbol of heaven and earth. A containing elegance tumbles down from heaven. It indicates a wonderful and creative time.

Nine above: Coupling with your horns, a trial of strength. This brings shame, though no serious harm. Being on top will exhaust you.

45 CLUSTERING, T'SUI

Keywords: Gather, assemble, animate. A great effort brings great rewards.

Clustering shows collecting and gathering. Unite people and things through a common goal. This is the time for great projects. The spirits will give you success, power and maturity. Be like the king who imagines a temple. Visit those who can help and advise you. Organize your thoughts. A great offering opens the Way. Having a direction brings profit and insight.

Cluster, T'sui: Gather, call or pack together; groups of people, animals and things; assemble, concentrate, collect, reassemble; crowd, multitude. The ideogram suggests gathering the capacity to do things.

The hexagram shows common labour coming to expression. The mists rise over the earth. Clustering means assembling and reuniting. Eliminate the need for weapons by being alert. Don't be taken by surprise. Clustering implies collecting people to work together. Be like the king who imagines building a temple. Think about your central idea. Correct how things come together. Making a great sacrifice opens the Way. Having a direction brings profit and insight. Yield and work with the heavenly mandate. You will see the motives of heaven, earth and the myriad beings.

TRANSFORMING LINES

Initial six: You are connected to the spirits and they will carry you through. At first things will be thrown into disorder. Bring them together again. Call out. One small effort triggers joy and laughter. Have no cares. Going on like this is not a mistake.

Six at-second: Prolonging the time opens the Way. Wait until you feel connected to the spirits, then proceed with your plan. Make an offering, even if your resources are thin.

Six at-third: As soon as there is clustering, there is sorrow and mourning. Having a direction brings no advantage here. Move on. This is not a mistake. If you try to adapt, you will only be humiliated.

Nine at-fourth: Take action. The Way to the Source is open. It is not a mistake.

Nine at-fifth: A cluster of people according to rank. There is no connection to the spirits in this group. This is not your fault. Divine for the connection again and again. This will extinguish your regrets.

Six above: You are paying for this connection with sighs and tears and sniffles. The house is not tranquil. You are surrounded by the wrong people. Do you really want to pay this price?

46 ASCENDING, SHENG
Keywords: Don't worry. Make the effort. Climb the mountain step by step.

升

Ascending describes your situation in terms of rising to a higher level and getting something done. Set a goal and work towards it step by step. Root yourself and push towards the heights. Climb the mountain and connect with the spirits. Bring out the hidden potential. The spirits will give you growth, power and maturity. See those who can help and advise you. Look at the great in yourself. Have no cares. Set to work. The Way is open. Put things in order.

LEFT THE 46TH HEXAGRAM
SHENG, OR ASCENDING, IS
ASSOCIATED WITH ACHIEVING
GOALS STEP BY STEP, AS
IF SLOWLY CLIMBING UP
A MOUNTAIN.

Ascend, Sheng: Mount, go up, rise; advance through your own efforts; be promoted, rise in office; accumulate, fulfil the potential; distil liquor; an ancient measure, a small cupful, thus bit by bit.

The hexagram shows adaptability rising from roots in the earth. Earth's centre gives birth to the tree. If you let yourself be led, you can realize your hidden potential. When people assemble and set a higher goal, they call it ascending. This success doesn't simply come to you. Yield to the impulse and work hard. Amass small things to reach what is great. Be adaptable. Penetrate to the core. The great spirits will give you success, power and maturity. Have no cares. You will obtain rewards. Take action. The Way is open. Put things in order. Your purpose is indeed on the move.

TRANSFORMING LINES

Initial six: Permitted to ascend the sacred mountain. Be honest and true. The Way is open. You are united with the higher powers.

Nine at-second: Connect with the spirits and put yourself in order. Make an offering, no matter how meagre your resources. You will soon have cause to rejoice.

Nine at-third: You ascend into an empty city. Don't stop now. This isn't the time to have doubts. Push on!

Six at-fourth: The king sacrifices on the mountain of Ch'i and presents you to the ancestors. Dedicate your energy to the good of the group. This opens the Way. It will certainly yield benefits for all.

Six at-fifth: The Way is open. Ascend the steps to the seat of power. Your purpose will make great gains.

Six above: Dim ascending with no lights to guide you. Don't stop now. The only way out is to keep going through it.

47 CONFINING/OPPRESSED, K'UN
Keywords: Look within. Find a way to break out of the trap.

Confining shows being cut off, oppressed and exhausted. You must collect the energy to break out and re-establish communication. The spirits will give you success, power and maturity. Be great and master the situation from within. Find what is truly important. The Way is open. The situation is not your fault. You are not believed when you speak. Don't believe what others are telling you.

Confine/Oppression, K'un: Enclosed; restrict, limit; punishment, penal codes, prison; anxiety, fear, fatigue, exhaustion, at the end of your resources; afflicted, disheartened, weary; poverty. The ideogram shows a tree growing in an enclosure.

The hexagram shows relations disconnected from the inner flow. The mists outside the stream. Hidden within the situation is the possibility of finding true help and encouragement. Separate your virtue from the collective values that oppress you. Bring old relations to an end. Don't be bound by grudges or bitter feelings. Find the mandate for change hidden here and use it to release your purpose. It is dangerous to express yourself now. Don't let go. The spirits will give you success, power and maturity. This opens the Way. Seek those who can help you. Find what is great. Believing what your oppressors tell you will only exhaust you.

TRANSFORMING LINES

Initial six: Buttocks oppressed by a wooden rod. Punished or hurt, you enter a dark valley, hiding in melancholy. Don't act like this! You will be cut off and alone for three years.

Nine at-second: Oppressed when drinking and eating – the oppression of not being recognized. Honour and accomplishment are on their way, coming at you from all sides. Connecting to the inner sources of energy brings profit and insight. Disciplining people or setting out on an expedition will close the Way.

Six at-third: Oppression is turning you to stone. All you see is thorns and snares. You walk into your house and don't see your helpmate. The Way is closed.

Nine at-fourth: Help is coming very slowly. When it arrives, you will realize you have been going at things the wrong way. It will bring this oppression to an end. You will soon have people to associate with.

Nine at-fifth: Oppressed by authority, your nose and feet are cut off. You will slowly find a way to express yourself. Connecting to inner sources of energy brings profit and insight. You haven't found your purpose yet.

Six above: Oppressed by creeping plants, stumbling towards danger. Why blather on, stirring up anguish and repenting? Set things in order. Discipline yourself and the Way will open.

48 THE WELL, CHING
Keywords: Communicate, connect, draw on the water.

The Well describes your situation in terms of an underlying social structure and the natural force that flows through it. The way to deal with it is to clarify and renew your connection to the source. The water is there for all to draw on, but the well that gives you access to it must be cleaned and maintained. You can change where you live and who you associate with, but you can't change the well and the needs it represents. Losing and acquiring, coming and going, all are part of the well and its water. If all you find is mud in the well, you haven't gone deep enough. Your rope is too short. If you ruin the pitcher used to draw the water, you will be cut off from the spirits and left open to danger.

The Well, Ching: A water well; the well at the centre of a group of nine fields; resources held in common; underlying structure; nucleus; in good order, regularly; communicate with others, common needs; the water of life, the inner source. The ideogram portrays a group of nine fields with the well at the centre.

The hexagram figure shows inner penetration flowing out into the world. Above wood there is the stream. Turn potential conflict into creative tension. When what is above is confined, what is below will reverse itself. The well means interpenetrating and free communication. It is the earth in which the power to realize the Way is grounded. It means staying where you are but shifting your ideas by differentiating what is right. Work for the common good at humble tasks. This encourages fortunate meetings. Inner penetration reaches to the stream and brings it to the surface. The well nourishes without being exhausted. You can change where you live, but you can't change the well. It is the solid centre. If you only bring up mud, your rope isn't long enough. You haven't achieved anything yet. If you ruin the pitcher used to hold the water, you will be cut off from the spirits and left open to danger.

TRANSFORMING LINES

Initial six: This well is a bog. You can't drink the water. It is an old source that no creatures come to. Time has left it behind. Wait for the right moment to act. Turn potential conflict into creative tension. If you let yourself be led, you can realize your hidden potential. The situation is already changing.

Nine at-second: This well is a gully in which you shoot fish. The pitcher that holds the water is cracked and leaking. There is no possibility of associating with others by using this source. Re-imagine the situation. Gather your energy for a decisive new move.

Nine at-third: This well is turbid because it is not being used. Your heart aches, because your capacities are not being drawn on. The water could be used if the person in control were bright enough to understand the situation. This shows someone of value unappreciated and under-employed. Although it hurts to move, seek out a situation in which your worth is recognized. This can bring blessings to all concerned. Take the risk. Provide what is needed. Be open to new ideas.

Six at-fourth: This well is being lined. Although the water can't be used, adjusting the source is not a mistake. This is a time of transition. Don't be afraid to act alone. You are connected to a creative force.

97

Nine at-fifth: There is cool, pure spring water flowing in this well. You can take it in. This source is central and correct. Make the effort. If you let yourself be led, you can realize your hidden potential. The situation is already changing.

Six above: This well receives everything and gives to everyone. Don't cover it up. Don't hide the source of value. You are linked to the spirits and they will carry you through. This is the source of great good fortune and meaningful events. You can accomplish great things. Gently penetrate to the core of the situation. Turn potential conflicts into creative tensions. The situation is already changing.

49 SKINNING/REVOLUTION, KO
Keywords: Strip away the old. Revolt and renew.

革

Skinning shows stripping away the protective cover. Radically change things. Eliminate what has grown old. You must wait for the right moment, when the snake sheds its skin. You will be linked to the spirits and they will carry you through. This begins a whole new cycle of time. Don't doubt it.

LEFT THIS FIGURE SUGGESTS SHEDDING OLD IDEAS AS A SNAKE SHEDS ITS SKIN.

Skin/Revolution, Ko: Moult, renew, revolt, overthrow; eliminate, repeal, cut away; leather armour, soldiers. The ideogram shows an animal skin stretched on a frame.

The hexagram shows changing awareness coming to expression. Fire in the middle of the mists. Reject old motives and quarrels. Change the measures of time. Wait for the right moment. Then act and trust what you are doing. You will be linked to the spirits and they will carry you through. Don't doubt. Heaven and earth renew themselves and the seasons accomplish things. Great people renew the mandate of heaven. Let serving connect you to heaven and resonance connect you to people. The time of skinning is truly great.

Transforming Lines
Initial nine: Bound and held fast with leather thongs. It is impossible to act now. Be open to the impulse when it comes.

Six at-second: This is the hour when the snake sheds its skin. Put things in order and act. The Way is open.

Nine at-third: Disciplining people and setting out now will close the Way. You are facing an angry old ghost. Wait until you hear people's inspiring words three times. Then act. You will be linked to the spirits and they will carry you through.

Nine at-fourth: Act now and have no doubts. You are linked to the spirits and they will carry you through. Change the mandates of heaven. The Way is open.

Nine at-fifth: When heaven changes, great people transform like tigers. Their fierce energy protects them. You are linked to the spirits and they will carry you through. Don't look for signs and omens.

Six above: When heaven changes, the noble person transforms like a panther, with grace and beauty. Small people simply change their faces. Stay where you are. The Way is open. Punishing people will close the Way.

50 THE VESSEL/HOLDING, TING
Keywords: Find an image. Hold and transform your problem in the vessel.

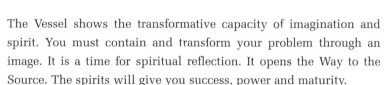

The Vessel shows the transformative capacity of imagination and spirit. You must contain and transform your problem through an image. It is a time for spiritual reflection. It opens the Way to the Source. The spirits will give you success, power and maturity.

Vessel/Holding, Ting: A cauldron, a sacred vessel for offerings, sacrifices and ritual meals; founding symbol of a family or dynasty; hold, contain and transform; consecrate, connect with the spirits; found, establish, precious, well-grounded. The ancient ideogram shows questioning the spirits.

The hexagram shows inner penetration feeding radiance and clarity. Above wood there is fire. Through the vessel you grasp renewal. Correct the situation to give your fate a solid base. The vessel means using symbols. The sage uses this to present things to the spirits above and nourish worthy people. The spirits will give you success, power and maturity.

TRANSFORMING LINES

Initial six: Turn the vessel upside down to clear the obstruction. This brings profit and insight, like taking a concubine when your wife can't have a child. This is not a mistake.

Nine at-second: There is food in the vessel. Your companions are resentful but they can't harm you. Accept this separation. It opens the Way. Bring your plan to completion without going to extremes.

Nine at-third: You must skin the vessel's ears. Things feel all clogged up now. You can't get at the juice. This is part of renewing how you understand the things of the spirit. Change will soon fall like rain and wash away your doubts and sorrows. Bringing your current plan to completion opens the Way.

Nine at-fourth: Breaking off the vessel's foot. This is wrong. Don't do it. You will betray what supports you. Everything will be soiled. The Way is closed.

Six at-fifth: This vessel has golden handles and metal rings. Your plans are cooked. You have found the centre. Putting your ideas to the trial brings profit and insight.

Nine above: You have found something precious in the vessel. This opens the Way to the Source. There is nothing this will not benefit. It articulates a whole new world.

51 SHAKE/AROUSING, CHEN
Keywords: The shock of the new. Stir things up. Don't get flustered.

Shake shows a disturbing and inspiring shock. Rouse things to new activity. Let the shock begin something new. Don't lose your concentration. What at first seems frightening will soon be a cause to rejoice. The spirits will give you success, power and maturity. The thunder rolls and people cry out, then you hear laughing and joyous talk. Although shock spreads fear for 30 miles, you hold the libation cup calmly so the dark wine calls the spirits.

Shake, Chen: Arouse, inspire, wake up, shake up; frighten, awe, alarm; violent thunder clap, earthquake; majestic, severe; excite, influence, break through the shell, come out of the bud. The ideogram shows the fertilizing rain.

The hexagram shows repeated shocks that stir things up. Reiterating thunder. Shake means stirring things up and beginning anew. Inspect and adjust yourself. The spirits will give you success, power and maturity. The shake terrifies everyone, but this anxiety soon brings blessings. It startles what is far away and frightens what is near. Don't lose your concentration. It is time to attend to the ancestral temple, the field altar and sacrifice to the gods of crops. Act as master of the ceremonies that bring fertility.

TRANSFORMING LINES

Initial nine: The shake comes, terrifying everyone. Then laughing words ring out. The Way is open. The anxiety brings you blessing. Let it move you. You will soon have all you need.

Six at-second: The shake releases an angry old ghost. Climb the mountain of transformation. Don't run after what you have lost. Everything returns to you on the seventh day.

Six at-third: The shake revives everything. Move with this impulse. It is not a mistake. Your current situation is not appropriate for you.

Nine at-fourth: The shake releases a bog. This impulse to act will trap and confuse you. The situation is not clear yet. Beware. Be open to new ideas. Don't take the lead.

Six at-fifth: The shake comes and goes. The impulse is unsteady. It releases an angry old ghost. You are moving through danger in an exposed position. If you stay intent on your idea, you will have plenty to do. Focus on your central concern and you won't get lost.

Six above: The shake is exhausted in demands and obligations. You watch this happening and are terrified. Don't try to discipline people and put things in order. The Way will close. Let it affect your neighbours and watch what is happening. That is not a mistake. Beware of words proposing marriages and alliances. There is a trap here, but you can avoid getting caught. Let what happened to your neighbours be a warning.

52 BOUND/STABILIZING, KEN
Keywords: The time comes to an end. Calm, still, stabilize, articulate.

Bound shows limits. Calm your desires. Stabilize your spine so you are not caught in compulsive actions. Move through life as if other people and their compulsive needs were not there. This is not a mistake. It allows you to articulate yourself.

Bound/Stabilizing, Ken: Limit, boundary; stop, still, quiet, calm, refuse to advance; enclose, confine, finish, complete; reflect on what has come before; firm, solid, simple, straightforward; the mountain as limit and refuge. The ideogram suggests turning around to see what has led to the present situation.

The hexagram shows the limit of things. You can't stir things up forever. Think things over deeply. Stir things up or quiet them at the right time. Then the Way shines brightly. Bound means staying in your place. Don't get your personality entangled in things. Move through your life as if other people were not there. Free yourself from error and make no further mistakes.

TRANSFORMING LINES

Initial six: Stabilize your feet. Make your foundation firm. This is not a mistake. It is a source of profit and insight.

Six at-second: Stabilize your calves. Stop moving. You can't rescue the people who follow you. Your heart does not rejoice at this. But don't stop listening to your inner voice.

Nine at-third: Trying to stabilize things, you freeze your hips and lower back, cutting yourself in half. This is repression. It releases an old angry ghost. Acrid smoke smothers your heart. This is definitely not how to put things in order.

Six at-fourth: Stabilize your personality. This is not a mistake. It frees you from errors. This means stopping your body's compulsive desires and reactions.

Six at-fifth: Stabilize your jaws. The words you speak will have order. Your doubts will be extinguished.

Nine above: Stabilize your boundaries. Be magnanimous. This opens the Way. Use these qualities to bring your plans to completion and you will meet them in others.

53 GRADUAL ADVANCE, CHIEN   漸
Keywords: Proceed smoothly, step by step. Don't take control.

Gradual Advance shows how to gradually achieve a goal. Advance slowly with subtle penetration. Move through the woman and the yin. Don't try to dominate. Through infiltrating, you find the place where you belong. Proceed step by step. This opens the Way. You will achieve mastery and find a field of activity. Putting your ideas to the trial brings profit and insight.

Gradual Advance, Chien: Advance by degrees, slowly and surely; pour into, flow into, permeate; influence, affect; smooth, gliding. The ideogram shows water penetrating things.

The hexagram shows an inner limit that stabilizes growth. A tree above the mountain. Be like a woman given in marriage who waits for the man's move. Depend on your inner power and virtue to improve the situation. By moving through yin and the woman you achieve mastery and a field of activity. Correct yourself in order to advance. Stabilize your desire and be adaptable. Gently penetrate to the core of the situation. The new energy that is stirring will not be exhausted.

TRANSFORMING LINES

Initial six: Wild geese advance to the river bank. A relationship begins. You are like a young child confronting difficulties. There is an angry old ghost here. Use words to deal with it.

Six at-second: Wild geese advance to the stone. The relationship is grounded. There is a feast in which everyone rejoices. This opens the Way.

Nine at-third: Wild geese advance to the dry plateau. The husband goes on campaign and does not return. The wife is pregnant and gives no support. The relationship breaks down. Acting like this closes the Wa violent and bruta your mutual prote

RIGHT THIS FIGURE
SUGGESTS SLOW ADVANCE,
LIKE A TORTOISE.

Six at-fourth: Wild geese advance to the trees. Perhaps you acquire a roof over your head. This is a good temporary solution. It is not a mistake. By yielding and serving you can adapt to the situation.

Nine at-fifth: Wild geese advance to the grave mound. The couple seeks the advice of the spirits. The wife will not conceive for three years. In the end nothing will hold you back. Don't try to complete things quickly. It is worth the time and effort. This opens the Way.

Nine above: Wild geese advance to the high plateau. Their feathers are used in rites and dances that connect with the fundamental powers. This opens the Way. The journey ends in the world of the spirits.

54 MARRYING THE MAIDEN, KUEI MEI
Keywords: Realize hidden potential. Let yourself be led.

Marrying the Maiden shows a change you must go through. Accept it and let yourself be led. It is moving you towards the place where you belong. Don't try to take control. That will close the Way. In the long run this leads to great success.

Marry/Convert, Kuei: Return to, change form; restore, revert, become loyal; to give a young girl in marriage. The ideogram shows a woman becoming head of a household.

Maiden, Mei: A young girl, a virgin; the younger or second sister. The ideogram shows a woman and the sign for not yet.

The hexagram shows self-expression following rousing energy. Above the mists there is thunder. Convert hidden potential through the woman and the yin. Don't try to dominate. Adapt and provide what is needed. You will soon understand what is unfit to be used. This is both an end and a beginning. If heaven and earth did not mingle, the myriad beings would never emerge. Stir up expression and pleasure. Punishing people or imposing your will closes the Way. Be adaptable and ride on the strong, solid force.

TRANSFORMING LINES

Initial nine: The maiden marries as a second wife. A lame person is able to make their way. Accept a secondary position cheerfully. It brings success in the end. Set things in order. The Way is open.

Nine at-second: By squinting you can really see things. Take an independent perspective. Solitude and obscurity bring profit and insight. Stay in the shade.

Six at-third: The maiden marries through waiting. Have patience. If you accept a secondary position now, you will turn the whole situation upside down. The time is not right.

Nine at-fourth: The date for the marriage has gone by. Draw out the time and act at your leisure. Wait for the right moment. But don't be idle within yourself.

Six at-fifth: The Great Ancestor gives a maiden in marriage. What comes from the womb of the first wife is not as fine as what comes from the womb of the second wife. This is an omen of ultimate success and happiness. Be like the moon that is almost full. The Way is open. You are located in the centre of things. Value your ability to move and act independently.

Six above: A woman offers a basket with nothing in it. A man sacrifices a goat with no blood. This is a sterile marriage; these are empty forms. There is no advantage in this situation. There is nothing honest or sincere at the top.

55 ABOUNDING, FENG

**Keywords: Shine on everything.
Give with no cares.**

Abounding shows abundance and fertile profusion. Be exuberant and expansive. Give with both hands. The spirits will give you success, power and maturity. Imagine yourself as the king whose power bestows wealth and happiness. Rid yourself of sorrow, melancholy and care. Be like the sun at midday. Shed light on all.

Abounding, Feng: Fertile, plentiful, copious, numerous; exuberant, prolific, overflowing; full, culmination; ripe, sumptuous, luxurious, fat; many talents, friends, riches. The ideogram shows a horn of plenty.

The hexagram shows brightness and warmth permeating the world. Thunder and lightning culminate. Assemble all your force. Abounding refers to a great idea. There are many causes for this. Cut through complications. Imagine yourself as a king whose power confers benefits on everyone. Rid yourself of sorrow and melancholy. Shed your light on everything. When the sun reaches the centre, it begins to set. When the moon becomes full, it begins to wane. Heaven and earth fill and empty all things. There is a time to build things up and a time to let things dissolve. This is even more true of people and the spirits that govern the world.

TRANSFORMING LINES

Initial nine: You meet your lord as an equal, someone who can help and teach you. You can continue in this relation. It is not a mistake.

Six at-second: Abounding screens and protects you. At noon you can see the great star constellation. If you act directly on your insight, you will be distrusted and injured. Trust your connection to the spirits to carry you forward and display your worth. This opens the Way. Trust in the connection to the inner world.

Nine at-third: Abounding flows in all directions. At noon, you can see the heavens full of stars. You break your right arm. This is an influx of extraordinary perception. You lose the capacity to act directly. This is not your fault. It is not a mistake to yield to the profusion.

Nine at-fourth: Abounding screens you and protects you. At noon you can see the great star constellation. You meet your lord in hiding, someone who can help and teach you. Together you can take action to change your situation. The Way is open.

Six at-fifth: The coming composition, a new chapter in the book of life, will bring you praise and rewards. The Way is open.

Six above: You use abounding to screen off your dwelling and peep out through the door, cutting yourself off from people. This cuts you off from the spirits and leaves you open to danger. If you go on like this, you will be isolated and alone for three years. What are you trying to conceal?

56 SOJOURNING/QUEST, LÜ
Keywords: Journeys, voyages, searching alone and outside.

Sojourning shows wandering journeys and living apart. You are outside the normal network, on a quest of your own. You must be small and flexible. Adapt to what crosses your path. The spirits will give you success, power and maturity. Be willing to travel and search alone. Put your ideas to the trial. The Way is open.

Sojourn/Quest, Lü: Travel, journey, voyage; stay in places other than your home; visitor, lodger, guest; a troop of soldiers, a group of travellers with a common goal; a stranger in a strange land. The ideogram shows people loyal to a symbol of something distant.

LEFT THE 56TH DIVINATORY FIGURE IS LINKED TO TRAVELLING AND JOURNEYS, PARTICULARLY SOLITARY JOURNEYS.

The hexagram shows an inner limit that stabilizes changing awareness. Fire above the mountain. Don't be afraid to act alone. You must let go of where you now live. Use your travels to connect solitary individuals. Make clear decisions even if they are painful. Being small and adaptable is pleasing to the spirits. Limit your desires when you join with others. This makes you aware of things. Put your ideas to the trial. The Way is open. The time of sojourning is truly and righteously great.

TRANSFORMING LINES

Initial six: The voyage breaks up into little pieces before it starts. You are being obnoxious and petty. If you go on like this, you will lose what security you have. Your purpose exhausted before you start.

Six at-second: The traveller approaches a resting place. Take care of your goods. You will acquire a young helper. Bring your plan to completion without going to excess.

Nine at-third: The traveller burns down the resting place and loses the young helper. You face an angry old ghost. You will be injured if you are pulled into the conflict. Don't be so self-righteous.

Nine at-fourth: The traveller obtains goods, an office and the signs of respect. Your heart is not glad. You haven't found yourself.

Six at-fifth: You shoot the golden pheasant with one arrow. You acquire praise and a mandate from on high.

Nine above: The bird burns its nest. Travellers laugh at first, then burst out crying. Do not act like this! You will lose all your property and the place where you rest. The Way is closed. Your own self-righteousness will defeat you.

57 GENTLY PENETRATING, SUN

Keywords: Gently penetrate to the core of the problem.

Gently Penetrating shows penetrating to the core of the problem by being supple and adaptable. Enter from below. Let the situation shape you. Adapt to whatever crosses your path, like the wind or the roots of growing plants. The spirits will give you success, power and maturity. Hold on to your purpose. Have a direction. See those who can help and advise you. This brings profit and insight.

Gently Penetrating, Sun: Enter into, put into; supple, mild, subtle; submit freely, be shaped by; support, foundation, base; wind, weather; wood, trees, growing plants. The ideogram shows a base from which things grow.

The hexagram shows subtle penetration over time. Following winds. It means being humble and hiding your virtues, paring away the unnecessary to find the Way. Evaluate things in private. Balance opposing forces. Be supple and adaptable to work with the strong. Have a direction on things. See those who can help and advise you. Think about the great in yourself and organize your thoughts. All these bring profit and insight.

LEFT THIS HEXAGRAM REPRESENTS THE ENERGY OF TREES AND OTHER GROWING PLANTS.

TRANSFORMING LINES

Initial six: Don't be indecisive in advancing and retreating. Whichever direction you take, be like a warrior. If you are indecisive, you will harm your own purpose. Putting your ideas to the trial brings profit and insight.

Nine at-second: Penetrate beneath the bed. Get to the core of this old story. Use shamans and read old histories. Bring it to light. This opens the Way. It is not a mistake. Get to the centre of the problem.

Nine at-third: Penetrating and pushy, you make incessant demands. Don't go on like this. Your purpose will be exhausted.

Six at-fourth: Take action. All your regrets disappear. You will catch three kinds of game in the hunt. You are in a position to achieve something solid.

Nine at-fifth: Put your ideas to the trial. The Way is open. All your doubts will vanish. There is nothing this will not benefit. Take three days to prepare before the fruit emerges, and three days afterwards to make sure things are in order.

Nine above: Stop trying to penetrate beneath the bed. You will lose your goods and your position. The Way is closed. You have taken your attempt to correct things too far.

58 OPEN/EXPRESSING, TUI

Keywords: Express yourself. Join with others. Persuade, inspire, enjoy.

Open shows communication, pleasure and exchange. Express yourself openly and interact with others. Cheer people and urge them on. Talk, bargain, barter, exchange information. Enjoy yourself and free others from constraint. The spirits will give you success, power and maturity.

Open/Expressing, Tui: Interface; interact, interpenetrate; express, persuade, stir up, urge on; cheer, pleasure, enjoy, responsive, free; meet, gather, exchange, trade; spoken words; mists, vapours rising from a marsh or lake that fertilize and enrich. The ideogram shows a person speaking.

The hexagram shows expression and interaction. The mists come together. Open means stimulating things through expression, being visible and visiting people. Join with friends to discuss and practise. Put your ideas to the trial through expressing them and urging people on. Yield and serve heaven by connecting with others. If you explain things to people, they will forget how hard they work. If you explain why something is difficult, they will even face death willingly. By explaining your central idea, you encourage people at their tasks.

112

TRANSFORMING LINES

Initial nine: Harmonizing through expression. Bring things together. Unite and adjust. The Way is open. Have no doubts.

Nine at-second: Expressing your ideas links you to the spirits and they will carry you through. The Way is open. Trust your purpose.

Six at-third: An opportunity is coming. Beware! This is not the right opening for you. The Way is closed. This situation is not appropriate.

Nine at-fourth: Expressing yourself through bargaining and arguing. You have not yet reached an agreement. Rigorously guard against sudden emotional afflictions that would distort your judgement. This gives you cause to rejoice.

Nine at-fifth: Strip away your old ideas. You are linked to the spirits and they will carry you through. You confront an angry old ghost. Correcting the situation is definitely the right thing to do.

Six above: Draw things out by expressing your ideas. The situation isn't clear yet. Make your way carefully.

59 DISPERSING, HUAN
Keywords: Clear away what is blocking the light.

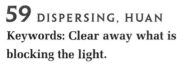

Dispersing shows how to eliminate misunderstandings, illusions and obstacles. Clear away what is blocking the light. Scatter the clouds, melt the ice, dispel fear and illusions, eliminate suspicions. The spirits will give you success, power and maturity. Be like the king who imagines a temple that connects people to the great spirits. Enter the stream of life with a purpose. Putting your ideas to the trial brings profit and insight.

Disperse, Huan: Scatter clouds, break up obstacles, dispel illusions, fears and suspicions; clear up, dissolve resistance; untie, separate; mobilize what is rigid; melting ice, floods, fog lifting. The ideogram suggests changing form by expanding or scattering.

The hexagram shows movement gently penetrating the world. The wind moves above the stream. Dispersing means letting the light shine through. Early kings used this to make offerings to the highest powers. The spirits will give you success, power and maturity. Be like the king who imagines a temple to connect with the great spirits. Enter the stream of life with a purpose. Make ready your vehicle and achieve something solid.

TRANSFORMING LINES
Initial six: Rescue this with the strength of a horse. The Way is open. Yield to the impulse and produce results.

Nine at-second: Disperse the obstacles by letting go of your habitual support. You will acquire what you desire.

113

Six at-third: Dispersing your identification with your body. Don't let your desires or your need to express yourself get in the way of what you are doing. Have no doubts about this.

Six at-fourth: Disperse your flock. The Way to the Source is open. Go to the hilltop shrine used to worship the spirits. It will give you a chance to ponder what is really significant. A great idea will come shining through.

Nine at-fifth: An order from on high. Sweat this one out. The king is moving his residence and you are part of the project. This is not a mistake. It will correct your situation.

Nine above: Disperse the bad blood. Remove the possibility of conflict. This is not a mistake. Keep harm at a distance by removing temptations.

114

60 ARTICULATING, CHIEH
Keywords: Articulate your thoughts. Set limits. Give things rhythm and form.

Articulating shows creating clear relations between things. Make connections clear. Express your thoughts. Separate and distinguish things. Make chapters, sections, units of time. Create a whole in which each thing has its place. The spirits will give you success, power and maturity. Don't harm yourself or others with rules that are bitter and harsh.

LEFT THIS HEXAGRAM IS LINKED TO UNITS OF TIME.

Articulate, Chieh: Separate, distinguish and join things; express ideas in speech; chapter, interval, unit of time, rhythm; the months of the year; limits, regulations, ceremonies, rituals, feasts; measure, moderate, temper; firm, loyal, true; establish degrees, levels and classes. The ideogram shows the nodes on a stalk of bamboo.

The hexagram shows expression articulating the stream of events. The mists above the stream. Things must be articulated. Cut them to size and calculate the measures. Think about virtue before taking action. The spirits will give you success, power and maturity. Harsh limits will prevent you from putting your ideas to the trial. Express things, take action, take risks. This is the right time to articulate your situation. Heaven and earth articulate the four seasons and accomplish their aims. Articulate the measures and the times and property will not be injured, the people will not be harmed.

TRANSFORMING LINES

Initial nine: Don't leave the house. Stay inside your own world for now.

Nine at-second: If you don't step outside the way you usually act, the Way will close. The time is coming to an end. Don't let the opportunity to change slip through your fingers.

Six at-third: If you don't articulate things, you will always be mourning over painful memories. Think about it. Whose fault is all this confusion and sorrow?

Six at-fourth: Quietly articulate things. The spirits will give you success, power and maturity.

Nine at-fifth: Sweetly articulate things. The Way is open. Going on like this brings honour and recognition.

Six above: Harsh measures and bitter speech. This closes the Way. Have no doubt. It will exhaust you.

61 CONNECTING TO CENTRE, CHUNG FU

Keywords: Connect your inner and outer life. Be in accord with the spirits.

中孚

Connecting to Centre shows bringing your life into accord with the spirit. Make connecting the inner and the outer parts of your life your central concern. Be sincere, truthful, reliable. Empty your heart so that you can hear the inner voices. This will link you to the spirits and they will carry you through. The Way is open. Swim in it like a dolphin in the stream. Enter the stream of life with a purpose. Putting your ideas to the trial brings profit and insight.

Centre, Chung: Inner, central, calm, stable; put in the centre; balanced, correct; mediate, intermediary; the heart, the inner life; stable point that lets you face outer changes. The ideogram shows an arrow in the centre of a target.

Accord, Fu: Accord between inner and outer; sincere, truthful, verified, reliable; have confidence; linked to and carried by the spirits; take prisoners, capture spoils, be successful. The ideogram suggests being protected and making a capture.

The hexagram shows inner expression permeating the outer world. Above the mists is the wind. Connecting to Centre means being trustworthy. Think about legal actions before getting involved and put off serious judgements. Be flexible and adaptable within, so the strong can acquire the centre. Be like the dolphin, who swims the seas of the Way. Commit yourself to the waters. The Way is open. Enter the stream of life with a purpose. Put your ideas to the trial. That brings profit and insight and connects you with heaven above.

TRANSFORMING LINES

Initial nine: Taking precautions opens the Way. But if you are always thinking about someone else, you will never be at ease.

Nine at-second: A crane calls out from its hiding place. The young son echoes the cry. I have a loving cup. Come to me and I will pour it out. This connection transforms your heart's desire. Don't hesitate to answer the call.

Six at-third: You acquire an antagonist. You beat the drums to sound the attack, then you call for a cease-fire. You weep, then you laugh. There is very little you can do in this situation.

Six at-fourth: The moon is almost full. Cut yourself off from your team. This is not a mistake. By separating yourself and going your own way, you can connect with higher energies.

117

Nine at-fifth: Act on your ideas. You are linked to the spirits and they will carry you through. This will connect you with others as surely as links in a chain. This is not a mistake. It is the right time to correct your situation.

Nine above: The cry of a bird mounts to the heavens. This is arrogant empty talk. The Way is closed. Why go on like this?

62 SMALL EXCEEDING, HSIAO KUO

Keywords: Carefully adapt to each thing. Keep your sense of purpose.

Small Exceeding shows an overwhelming variety of details. Carefully adapt to each thing in turn. The spirits will give you success, power and maturity. Putting your ideas to the trial brings profit and insight. The time allows small things. It does not allow great things. The flying bird leaves the message: the above is not suitable, the below is suitable. The Way is open. Keep your sense of purpose. This is an important transition.

Small, Hsiao: Little, common; adapt to what crosses your path; take in, make smaller; dwindle, lessen; little, slim, slight; yin energy.

Exceed, Kuo: Go beyond, surpass, overtake, overshoot; get clear of, get over; cross the threshold, surmount difficulties; transgress the norms, outside the limits.

The hexagram shows an inner limit restricting new energy. Thunder above the mountain. Through being very small you can move through this transition. When you are active, be excessively polite. When you are mourning, be excessively sorrowful. When you are paying, be excessively frugal. The spirits will give you success, power and maturity. Putting your ideas to the trial brings profit and insight. Small matters are allowed. Great matters are not allowed. A flying bird leaves this message as a symbol: the above is not suitable, the below is suitable. The Way is open.

TRANSFORMING LINES
Initial six: The bird tries to fly. The Way is closed. Don't act like this.

Six at-second: Pass your grandfather by and meet your grandmother. Pass by the chief and meet the servant. Working from a secondary position is not a mistake. Make your heart small.

Nine at-third: You are in a perilous position. All you can do is defend yourself. If you push on, you risk death. The Way is closed.

Nine at-fourth: This is not a mistake. You meet the object of your desire. Let the difficulties that are now passing away be a warning to you. Don't keep trying to stay in the same place.

Six at-fifth: Dense clouds roll in from the West, but the rain hasn't arrived. The duke shoots a string-arrow and connects with someone in hiding. This is an enduring connection to a higher power.

Six above: You don't meet what you want, you pass it by, like the flying bird who leaves the earth far behind. The Way is closed. You invite calamity from within and without.

63 ALREADY
FORDING, CHI CHI
Keywords: Stay in the process. The situation is already changing.

Already Fording shows a process already underway. Go on with what you are doing, fording the stream of events. Things are in their proper places. Aid and encourage the process. The spirits will give you success, power and maturity. Putting your ideas to the trial brings profit and insight. Stay with the process. The Way is open. Trying to complete things creates disorder.

Already, Chi: Completed, finished; mark of the past tense. The ideogram shows a person having begun a meal.

Ford, Chi: Cross a river, overcome an obstacle, begin an action; give help, bring relief; succeed, complete, achieve. The ideogram depicts a shallow ford.

The hexagram shows clarity in action. The stream above the fire. Things are cooking. Gather your energy and put it at the service of the process. You are fording the stream. This means setting things right. Think deeply about the problems and prepare yourself. Adapt to whatever crosses your path. The spirits will give you success, power and maturity. You are in the right place. Correct the balance between things. Stay in the process. The Way is open. Completing things and stopping the action only creates disorder.

TRANSFORMING LINES

Initial nine: Pull your wheels back. Get your tail wet. You are starting too quickly. This is not a mistake.

Six at-second: A wife loses her veil. Don't chase what is gone. In seven days you will have it all back again.

Nine at-third: The Great Ancestor subdues demons on all sides. It will take three years to control their country. You will have to confront your own ghosts. Don't simply adapt to things. Keep on though you are weary and distressed.

Six at-fourth: Even silk clothes become rags in a single day. You are crossing the river in a leaky boat. Be constantly on guard.

Nine at-fifth: The eastern neighbour sacrifices a bull. The western neighbour makes a small offering. Sincerity is important here. By being true to yourself you receive the gifts of the spirits. The Way to the Source is open.

Six above: You soak your head. You are in too deep. You are confronting an angry old ghost and are not in the position to deal with it. Why let this go on?

64 NOT YET FORDING, WEI CHI

Keywords: Gather your energy for a decisive new move.

Not Yet Fording shows being on the verge of an important change. Gather your energy for this decisive new move. The possibilities are great. Be sure your plans are in order and that you can make the crossing without getting stuck. The spirits will give you success, power and maturity. Don't be like the small fox that almost gets across the river and then soaks her tail in the mud. That would leave you nowhere to go and nothing to help you.

Not Yet, Wei: Incomplete, doesn't exist yet; has not occurred. The ideogram shows a tree that has not yet extended its branches.

Ford, Chi: Cross a river, overcome an obstacle, begin an action; give help, bring relief; succeed, complete. The ideogram shows a shallow ford.

The hexagram figure shows the potential for order. Fire is located above the stream. Things aren't cooking yet. Things are moving towards their proper place. Life cannot be exhausted. The potential is always there. That is the meaning of Not Yet Fording. It implies diminishing masculine drive and gathering your energy for a decisive new move. The spirits will give you success, power and maturity. By being supple and adaptable you can acquire the central position. The small fox who crosses a river never lets go of her centre. If you start out, then soak your tail, there is nothing that can help you. The supple and the strong are acting in harmony to move you towards where you belong.

TRANSFORMING LINES

Initial six: You soak your tail. Too much, too soon. If you act this way, you show that you don't really understand.

Nine at-second: Pull your wheels back. Start slowly. The Way is open. Stay in the centre and correct how you are moving.

Six at-third: You are preparing for a decisive new move. Don't discipline or punish people. That closes the Way. Stepping into the stream of life with a purpose brings profit and insight.

Nine at-fourth: Put your ideas to the trial. This generates meaning and good fortune. The Way is open. Doubts and regrets will vanish. Invade the demon's country. After three years of hard work you will be rewarded in the capital. You will have to confront your own ghosts and shadows. Your purpose is truly moving.

Six at-fifth: Put your ideas to the trial. The Way is open. You will have no cause to regret this. Power and virtue shine through it. You are linked to the spirits and they will carry you through. You will be splendid in your good fortune.

Nine above: You are linked to the spirits and they will carry you through. Gather with others and celebrate. Soak your head so you can let go of the past.

FURTHER READING

Karcher, S, *How to Use the I Ching*, Element Books, Shaftesbury, 1997

A classic study:
Wilhelm, H, *Heaven, Earth and Man in the Book of Changes*, University of Washington Press, Seattle, 1977

A comprehensive list of books in English on the *I Ching*:
Hacker, E A, *The I Ching Handbook*, Paradigm Publications, Brookline, 1993

On the most important traditional teaching about using the *I Ching*:
Karcher, S, *Ta chuan: The Great Treatise*, St. Martin's Press, 2000

Peterson, W, 'Making Connections: Commentary on the Attached Verbalizations of the Book of Change', Harvard Journal of Asiatic Studies, 42/1, pp 67-112, June 1992

On divination:
Karcher, S, *The Illustrated Encyclopedia of Divination*, Element Books, Shaftesbury, 1997

A look at the depth psychological approach:
Jacobi, J, *Complex/Archetype/Symbol*, Princeton University Press, Princeton, 1974

Sources on Chinese history and traditional culture:
Allan, S, *The Way of Water and Sprouts of Virtue*, SUNY, Albany, 1997
Maspero, H, *China in Antiquity*, trans. Frank A. Kierman, University of Massachusetts Press, Amherst, 1978

The classic Confucian translation with an introduction by C. G. Jung:

Wilhelm R, and Baynes, C F, trans., *The I Ching or Book of Changes*, 3rd edition, Princeton University Press, Princeton, 1967

An interesting new translation of the oldest parts of the book:

Wu Jing-Nuan, *Yijing*, Taoist Study Series, Washington DC, 1991

A definitive sourcebook on the words and their many meanings:

Ritsema, R, and Karcher, S, *I Ching: The Classic Chinese Oracle of Changes*, Shaftesbury, Element Books, 1995

OTHER BOOKS OF INTEREST INCLUDE:

Kerson and Huang, R, *I Ching*, Workman, New York, 1985

Loewe, M, and Blacker, C, (eds), *Divination and Oracles*, Shambhala, Boulder, Colorado, 1981

Matthews, J, (ed.), *The World Atlas of Divination*, Headline, London, 1992

Sherrill, W A, and Chu, W K, *An Anthology of I Ching*, Routledge and Kegan Paul, London, 1977

Wing, R, *The I Ching Workbook*, Doubleday, New York, 1982

Useful Addresses

Stephen Karcher often runs workshops and courses in various places, and does individual consultations. For information contact him at:

8 Glan'rafon Bontuchaf
Carneddi
Bethesda
Bangor
LL57 3TB

The Oracle is a journal devoted to *I Ching* studies, mostly historical and scholarly, but of great interest. For information or subscription:

The Oracle
7 Hillend
Shooters Hill
London
SE18 3NH

Website: http://www.mension.com/oracle/index.htm

I Ching Bookmarks is a website that can connect you with several hundred other *I Ching* sites: http://www.zhouyi.com

Abounding 107–8
Adorning 55–6
Already Fording
119–20
answers 8, 12–18
Arguing 30–1
Arousing 100–2
Articulating
114–16
Ascending 92–3
associations 22
Attending 29–30
Augmenting 86–7

Biting Through
52–5
Bound 14, 102–3
Brightness Hiding
76–7

chance 8
Chen 100–2
Chi Chi 119–20
Chieh 114–16
Chi'en 23–4
Ch'ien 44–6
Chien 81–2,
103–5
Chin 75–6
China 9
Ching 95–7
Chou Dynasty 9
Chou I 9
Chun 26–7

Chung Fu
116–17
Clan 78–9
Clarifying 67–9
Clustering 90–2
coins 8, 15
complexes 9–10
Concording People
41–2
confining 94–5
Conjoining
69–70
Connecting to
Centre 116–17
Corruption
49–50
Coupling 89–90

de-personalization
6
Deciding 87–9
Deliverance 82–4
desires 18
Difficulties 81–2
Diminishing 84–5
Dispersing 17, 18,
113–14
Diverging 79–81
divination 9–10,
18–19
Divinatory Figures
17, 23–122
Dwelling People
78–9

empowerment 10
Enveloping 27–8
Eranos Foundation
6
Expressing 111–13

Feng 107–8
Field 13, 24–6
Following 47–9
Force 13, 23–4
Fu 58–9
Further reading
122–3

Gently Penetrating
110–11
Gnawing 52–5
goals 18
Gorge 14
Gradual Advance
103–5
Great Accumulating
61–2
Great Exceeding
64–5
Great Invigorating
73–5
Great Possessing
43–4
Grouping 33–4
guides 8

Han Dynasty 9, 12
Heng 71–2

hexagrams
divinatory figures
23–122
interpretation 7,
12–18
Key 19–21
Holding 99–100
Hsaio Kuo 117–19
Hsi K'an 66–7
Hsiao Ch'u 34–6
Hsieh 82–4
Hsien 69–70
Hsü 29–30
Huan 113–14
Humbling 44–6

inner beings 9–10
intuition 22

Jaws 63–4

Ken 102–3
Key 17, 19–21
Keywords 17
Ko 97–9
Kou 89–90
Ku 49–50
Kuai 87–9
Kuan 52–3
K'uei 79–81
Kuei Mei 105–6
K'un 24–6, 94–5

Leading 32–3
Legions 32–3
Li 67–9

Lin 50–2
Loosening 82–4
Lü 36–7, 108–10

magic 6, 19
marbles 8, 15–16
Marrying the
Maiden 105–6
mechanization 6
Meng 27–8
Ming Yi 76–7

Name 17, 18
navigation 8
Nearing 50–2
Not Yet Fording
120–2

Obstruction
39–41
Open 14, 111–13
Oppressed 94–5
oracles 6, 9–10,
18–19
origins 9

Penetrating 14
Persevering 71–2
Persisting 23–4
Pervading 38–9
Pi 33–4, 39–41,
55–6
planning 10
Po 56–8
Primary Hexagrams
16–17, 18

problem-solving
11–12
Prospering 75–6
Providing For
46–7
psychology
9–10, 19

Quest 108–10
questions 8,
11–12, 22

Radiance 14,
67–9
Relating Hexagrams
16–17, 18
Renovating
49–50
Repeating Gorge
66–7
repression 6
Retiring 72–3
Returning 58–9
Revolution 97–9

seeds 7, 8
Shake 14, 100–2
Sheng 92–3
Shih 32–3
Shih Ho 52–5
Skinning 97–9
Small Accumulating
34–6
Small Exceeding
117–19
Sojourning 108–10

soul-doctors 22
spirits 6, 7, 8, 9–10, 19
spiritual evolution 19
Sprouting 26–7
Stabilizing 102–3
Stripping 56–8
Sui 47–9
Sun 84–5, 110–11
Sung 30–1
Swallowing 63–4
symbols 8

Ta Ch'u 61–2
Ta Chuang 73–5
Ta Kuo 64–5
Ta Yu 43–4
T'ai 38–9

tao 7–8, 9, 10–12, 18–19
Ting 99–100
Transforming Lines 17, 18
Treading 36–7
trigrams 12–15
T'sui 90–2
Tui 111–13
Tun 72–3
T'ung Jen 41–2

Venturing 66–7
The Vessel 99–100
Viewing 52–3

Warring States period 9
way 7

Wei Chi 120–2
Welcoming 89–90
The Well 95–7
wills 7
Without Embroiling 59–61
Wu Hsien 9
Wu Wang 59–61

yang 15–16, 18
yarrow stalks 8, 9, 15
Yi 63–4, 86–7
Yielding 24–6
yin 15–16, 18
Yü 46–7